The Irresponsible Arts

The Irresponsible Arts

by William Snaith

Atheneum   New York   1964

Foreword

It is a disquieting thing to find one's attitude toward contemporary art has undergone a measure of sea change. Before, there always had been the conviction that through the pursuit and realization of modern art, one would find the grail at the end of the quest.

It is a change that takes place quietly, almost imperceptibly. Suddenly the moment comes when one is aware of a new set of opinions. With this awareness a private feeling of dismay intrudes into the consciousness. Can this be the onset of hardening of the intellectual arteries? Is this the classic transit from wide-eyed proselyte to curmudgeon?

The esthetic experience through the years did not seem discontinuous. The grand line from the exhilarating time when one discovered what Picasso was all about to the day when one stood in front of a Franz Kline, responding and reacting to his energy and power, yet feeling unsatisfied in the face of this private torture in paint—all of this time seems of a piece. No significant esthetic trauma had taken place, no revelations, no visions on a road to Damascus. Not even a complete disavowal was imminent.

And yet the fact remains that a distinct shift in personal attitude had taken place. A great deal of the reason lay in the broken promises of the esthetic rebellion —a rebellion once thought to be sacred to one's own generation and later discovered to be just a prolongation of one which had been going on for more than a century. Once such an act of rebellion meant a steppingstone to a bright new world, even if the act did nothing but destroy a piece of the old. But now we are engulfed in rebellion. It no longer seems to be going any place. It has become a habit, a fashionable posture. Goals once held are obscure or have entirely slipped away. It still is difficult to perceive this. We have been so involved with the judgment of the honesty and integrity of the artist that we have overlooked the need for honesty and integrity in the appreciator. One can collect styles just as one collects stamps, matchboxes or even string. But unless a man has the instincts of a pack rat or a historian, what has this to do with esthetic experience?

The past is ever present. At a moment when one begins to re-examine the basis for evaluation of current esthetics, then the past becomes the eternal Bureau of Standards, of weights and measures. But principally the past gives an assurance that art is noble and not just a pother of clever tricks. Curiously, this assurance does not exclude what one considers to be the deserving new art from the same exciting and pleasurable involvement, but rather provides a basis for a borderless appreciation not constrained to time or posture. This appreciation does not necessarily involve convictions as to its future place in art. With this it is possible to experience an intense esthetic relationship with musicians extending in a great line from Bach, Mozart, Beethoven, Wagner, Debussy, Stravinsky, Hindemith, Bartók, Schönberg and Varese. In architecture the feeling of awe at Chartres or Santa Sophia does not inhibit the thrill from seeing the Stockholm Town Hall or Wright's "Falling Water" or "Taliesen West," but does provide freedom from slavish acceptance of everything the master has done. It enables one to reject the ideas and designs which brought the Guggenheim Museum into being. And in painting, while still deeply involved with Cézanne, Picasso and Klee, one finds more human intensity and emotion compressed into a Byzantine icon than in all of the fustian of the abstract expressionist or in the over-blown comments of the pops men.

Yet, one cannot escape the feeling that in all this straining for effect lies a great potential. So much so that in making choices of the kind of art and artists to place in one's personal pantheon, it obviously is impossible to construct a list that not only meets everyone's approval, but is to the complete satisfaction of oneself. Such choices are subjective and personal. What makes it even more difficult is the fact that many artists are earnestly involved in areas of work for which one may have an instinctive response. If, for instance, one holds discipline to be an important aspect of art, then why cannot Joseph Albers be included in such a personal list, or for that matter Dali, and in quite another context, Mies van der Rohe with his high-rise buildings? In the end, one must agree or disagree with the purposes to which that discipline is applied. The great potential will be realized if the artists can find their way back to human purposes.

It is the latter quality that accounts for the continuity of the past and the viable present. It is the loss of that quality that accounts for the malaise which affects the attitude toward contemporary art. Beyond the questions which have arisen is a growing feeling of outrage over the idea that what is happening to art is part of the natural process of evolution and that this is good. It is not easy to reject ideas that most powerful voices keep reiterating. It is not even easy to organize one's protest against such a volume of praise.

It was sheer accident that a rereading of Juvenal took place when this feeling of inchoate outrage was in fomentation. Armed with the knowledge that protest against an accepted order was as old as history, I organized the reasons for my distress with certain proponents and aspects of contemporary art. Gratefully I dedicate this result to the spirit of Decimus Junius Juvenalis (who was able to last through ten emperors!) and take for my text the first and third lines from the first *Satire*.

Must I be listening always, and not pay them back? How
  they bore me. . . .
What license have they for this, their endless ranting and
  droning? [1]

[1] *The Satires of Juvenal,* trans. Rolfe Humphries (Bloomington:
Indiana University Press, 1958).

Contents

Part 1

Argument

The revolution in art which began more than a century ago rages on as fiercely as ever. It has not lost its steam—only its purpose. Art has become obsessed with originality, troubled by an advancing technology; it has destroyed its disciplines and turned its back on man.

The impetus for the revolution came from the artist's desires to express his concern about human experience with greater freedom. He had been constrained by the formal academies and the art establishment of the right. They are crushed, their power to influence gone. The art establishment is now of the left. The revolution has been won, its goals reached, but the revolution goes on. It now is revolution for revolution's sake, impelled by the whirlwind of its own momentum. It is not unlike a sociopolitical revolution which has gained its initial objectives, the destruction of oppression, but cannot find a way to turn its new freedoms into blessings.

This is not the first revolution in art. The history of art is the history of man's changing spiritual, esthetic and material aspirations. However, it now has reached a crucial point in its revolutionary history. For if it continues on its present course, art, or at least painting art, may become an esthetic indulgence, isolated and separate from the realities of existence. It will be maintained like some exotic laboratory culture, kept alive in a test tube, insulated and immunized from contact with the living, its future purpose unknown. This is one unhappy prospect for art. Or if man's genius for the survival of his institutions and himself still holds, perhaps art once again can be inextricably bound up with his needs, dreams and aspirations. But before this happens, the serious nature of man's separation from art must be reversed.

While the revolution in art came from the artist's desire for freedom, the source of the separation of man and art lies in the credo which electrified all artists shortly after the turn of the 19th century and is summed up in the "art for art's sake" slogan coined by Théophile Gautier and Charles Baudelaire. Beginning with such an intoxicating license to explore esthetic potentials never before tried, art steadily has moved away from conscious identification with human experience. The artist has become increasingly involved with the means by which he accomplishes his ends. The practice has reached a point wherein the means in themselves have become the sole purpose. The overwhelming importance of means over content is a phenomenon not restricted to a single art form. To the degree that the arts have characteristics in common, or permit any universality of esthetic experience, they share the same negative virtues. They are incomprehensible. They are noncommunicative. In areas such as architecture, where they intimately touch man, a higher virtue is placed on the fulfillment of esthetic goals than on the service of human needs. The arts, once an immediate reflection of men's spiritual responses, have withdrawn behind a veil of obscurantism. The lack of responsibility to men and of artists to themselves is hidden behind a bravura technical display and the clamor of the cults which surround them.

The estrangement of man and art is one facet of the alienated world we live in. The pace of that alienation was increased and its effects intensified in the last half-century. The sense of meaninglessness has grown. Man still is the troubled Am-Ha-Arez of Biblical times, but now without a Messiah. He sees the diminishment of himself on every hand. Once sovereign in his world, he watches a Frankenstein monster, progress, his own invention, rush on inexorably toward some goal of its own, pushing its creator aside.

Jeremiads are no longer in style, but any present-day

breast beating would entail a long and relentless account of the estate of man as his estrangement has grown.

He is being cut off from any meaningful contact with nature.

He is leaving the land to be herded into great impersonal cities.

He no longer knows the victory of a successful harvest in the face of storm, drought or flood.

He has lost the exultation of the successful hunt for his meat.

He has been robbed of his gods and beliefs by his own reasoning and science.

He has lost the glory in the strength of his arm, replaced by engine and machine.

He turns his back on the problems of his planet— hunger, shelter, pestilence, war—and looks to the planets Venus and Mars for answers.

His proud possession, his brain, is being displaced in many daily tasks by the electronic computer.

His exotic technology surpasses the physical capacity of his muscles and nervous responses, and he must depend on instruments to make decisions of control.

His machines are governed by machines while he idly sits by.

His diminishment increases.

He has lost his name to a serial number or dog tag, Social Security card and Diners' Club membership.

He has lost his oneness in the crowd and cannot see his contribution in a specialist and piece-work system.

He feels his sense of outrage blunted and reduced to

impotence by the mechanics of his society.

He finds his rewards and laurels in the benefits of the retirement fund.

His future is uncertain. One hand offers material promise, the other threatens to wipe him out.

His victories are gone, his sense of historic mission lost.

Thus, by the compulsion of historical development, without intention, man in his lust to get on has created a society crowded with things which back him into a narrowing corner.

Of all of the works of man, art has been the most consistent source of beauty and of spiritual enlargement, but the artist's response to mankind's general loss of self has been to turn his back on his role as communicator of beauty and human emotion. In a world he never made he addresses himself to an élite, a slim group of esthetes, mandarins and dilettantes who view his world through his own Coney Island mirror reflection. Together they have developed an elaborate set of esthetic rituals and mumbo-jumbo. Art has become a private set of ideographs to which ordinary people do not have the key. Communion with and enjoyment of art is denied them. The tragic result is that art has become an additional instrument of alienation.

Technique

The artist in his abandonment of human experience as a motivation has come to rely heavily on technique. He is torn between the surface imitation of the

symbols of the machine age in precise mechanical
works and conversely in works which are the very
antithesis of the mechanical image. In this latter category of art he employs automatism, improvisation and
accident. Such an art form relieves the artist from
responsibility, since the result is guided by an esthetic
Ouija board. The painter artist in this latter category
extends the nihilistic outrage with his society to art,
in the use of incompatible materials which are un-
stable or consume one another chemically so that the
life of his work is as transitory as he himself. The
sculptor with the same motivation explores the assembly of junk.

Musicians in this society, faced with an overwhelming past and the drive toward originality and self-
identity, have taken a leap into a strange new world.
With heavy reliance on technical means for motivation, they have cut an important umbilical cord, tonality, which until now has connected man and music,
and have organized their musical creativity around a
system which has little relationship to the music which
has furnished hymns, anthems and dirges. The avant-
garde has abandoned the employment of musical
instruments and voices and uses instead mechanically
produced electronic sounds and percussive noises,
sometimes haphazardly, at times in a mathematical
arrangement.

Architects have created a series of buildings which
essentially are conceived as hollow sculptures to which
people must adapt themselves. The critic Lewis Mumford has likened them to Procrustean beds. The esthetic motivation for these giant sculptures ranges

from a direct reflection of the machine age as seen in the coldly precise cubes of metal and glass to the exploration of expressionist concrete forms. We have come from the glass greenhouse to the concrete grotto.

Originality

All men are driven by a need for self-fulfillment. In the artist this need intensifies and couples with the compulsion for self-expression. Lacking the controlling discipline of the need to communicate, he has indulged in an unbridled use of originality. Originality, always a prime requirement in art (without it art would become hackneyed, stultified), has now reached a level of importance in the scale of values never before experienced. One contemporary critic, Harold Rosenberg, has labeled present-day art as the art of the new, declaring this to be its principal purpose and motivation. In the critical summation of a man's work the aspect which now receives the greatest consideration and scores most heavily is his originality. With the loss of other standards of value judgment heretofore employed—the values of beauty, nobility, communication—it is evident that originality (or perhaps more precisely stated, eccentricity) has become the paramount virtue in art. The net result has been an avalanche of excesses, indiscriminate and transitory, every new day's excess crowding out yesterday's. Faced with such a torrent of change and strangeness, ordinary man becomes even more baffled and hostile, so that the estrangement of man and art increases.

Art Establishment

The artist no longer fights a lonely battle. He is not isolated from the groups which dictate acceptance or rejection. His individual problem is rather to make a place for his particular brand of newness. The idea of the newness, however, is completely acceptable. The artist finds support for his course in the art establishment of today. This establishment, while not as simple and stratified as that which flourished under Napoleon III and his Minister of Fine Arts, is unified by a responsiveness to the new and a desire for separateness from ordinary man.

The establishment is made up of several segments of society motivated by a wide range of individual drives. In the establishment can be found esthetes whose basic appreciation and sensitivity mark them apart from the commonplace. Within it can be found the mandarins, a powerful élite, the self-appointed tastemakers, intellectually superior to the balance of the community and endowed with leadership instincts which set them at the head of the oligarchy of taste. In it, too, can be found those whose drives for separateness derive from their sexual estrangement from the normalcy of society. No small segment within the totality of the establishment is that of the status seekers, who use the inherent separateness of contemporary art as a *modus operandi* for establishing their assumed superior apartness and, by identifying themselves with other groups more esthetically endowed, are provided with a special posture. It is this latter well-heeled group of new art fanciers, who use contemporary art as a symbol of the good life and their possession of it as tantamount to their membership in the in-group, which largely supplies the funds to keep the whole establishment operative. Through their avid collections of the new art and support of the institutions, the museums and societies of the establishment, they pour considerable energy into the system. They may support the new art without demanding understanding, or necessarily liking it, because in its being new it is a symbol which identifies them with their time and with the leadership community. They use it as a decorative artifact in their homes and businesses. They make little other demands of it. If it is a house, it need not be livable; a chair, it need not be comfortable; a picture or a piece of sculpture, it need not be comprehensible. If it is music, it need not be fathomable or gratifying. It is enough that it is new.

These diverse groups are welded mainly by their mutually shared stimulation of the new and rare, by the organizations which they support, and by their self-conscious awareness that their superior knowledge and sensitivity divorces them from and sets them above the commonalty.

The Nature of the Estrangement

Thus, motivated by the philosophy of "art for art's sake" and impelled by an overwhelming technology, the imperative drive for originality, and the support of an isolated sector of society, the artist has arrived at his present attitude toward art. Avowedly he finds a collectivized and conformist society repugnant. In his desire to escape from identification with that society, and by the nature of his comments upon it, he has increased the very elements of estrangement of which he despairs and has left ordinary man more bereft and bewildered than ever.

The degree to which the ordinary man, even an informed man, resigns himself to the existence of an art which he cannot understand, but which rather eludes and baffles him, amounts almost to a belief in determinism. To him it is as though art had a will and direction of its own, free and independent of man; that somehow, mysteriously, within its corpus it contained a sort of historical imperative that drove it in a preordained direction. With this semi-belief it therefore follows that if art has become dehumanized and is unfortunately an additional factor of estrangement, then this misfortune, too, is accepted as predetermined.

This nonquestioning attitude has become more important in the last few decades as the artist and the establishment have arrogated to themselves the rights and privileges of Brahmans and put the role of untouchable on the balance of man. Man dare not speak out with any conviction or authority beyond complaint of his bewilderment. This attitude of passive compliance has been aided by the intellectual blackmail of past events. This subtle blackmail is grounded in the self-conscious fears of people who dare not voice disagreement with the art around them because they have witnessed the scorn heaped on the works of certain artists of the past, only to see these artists become revered and prophetic creators at a later day. When they do dare exercise their critical judgment, they are reminded that earlier generations, through a lack of understanding, rejected Monet, Cézanne and Van Gogh among many others. This is a powerful form of intellectual blackmail. It is enough to halt questioning at the outset. With this kind of evidence constantly recalled, it takes a great deal of courage to pick and choose with intellectual freedom. Obscured is the fact that at the very time that the now-revered artists were being scorned, it was the establishment of that day who did the rejecting. It had its own heroes who since have fallen on the trash heap of art history. Today's establishment brushes aside the errors of the earlier academy and asks to have its own judgments accepted as infallible. The difference between the academy of yesterday and that of today is that the old one was conservative and the present one is radical. The new academy happily is involved with the cult of the new at a time when the word "new" is probably the most influential word in use. At such a time and in such an atmosphere, it is difficult to recognize that this may be an important moment for taking stock and consolidating. In any case, the prevailing intellectual blackmail is used by the establishment to take on the rights of hierarchical judges. They are the interpreters of arts' laws, Sanhedrins with self-appointed rights.

In a brief span of years we have seen the passage of short-lived styles and movements, each vigorously supported by the art establishment at the time. Each has reigned with excitement, only to give way to a new wonder. The business of art today is conducted like that of a large monthly magazine, always searching for a big circulation-building sensation, each edition giving way in the next to another sensation, the idea of the discard hidden by the proclamation of the new.

Confronted by this sort of esthetic promotion, even the informed man has been made to feel that his lack of understanding is not only normal, but that it has ever been so; and his sense of resignation and acceptance of inevitability grow.

Toward an Informed Attitude

Art is not deterministic or governed by immutable or mysterious laws. It is made by men for men, and it is the men of art, the artists, who shape its direction. The present dehumanization of art is universal. It is not limited to a particular art form, for the same forces which turn an art into a cabalistic ritual are at work in each. The question of universality in the arts has been a point of discussion for many years. Philosophers have made extended analyses of the marriage of drama and opera, music and dance, sculpture and architecture. According to Susanne Langer, this is not so much a marriage as a rape. For the moment it is immaterial whether such a basis for universality exists or not. The central element of universality is the artist himself. Our society has had an impact on the artist and artists have influenced one another. It is the artist who, for utterly human reasons, has turned his back on his fellow man. It is he who has altered the relationship of art and man.

Art has been the great emotional language of man, the outward symbol of his inner feeling. Through the agency of the artist, it is man's comment upon and response to his world. It is his voice in hope and aspiration, in sorrow and despair. It is a source as well as a reflection of beauty, an adornment which has enriched his life with sensuous delight. It is the language of his spirit, inexpressible in any other way. When it stops being these things and becomes instead a private celebration for a few, antihuman if not anti-art, then man may well question whether it earns his continued love and respect. If it no longer recognizes his needs and desires, then does it deserve his support? When his godlike language which gave form and recognition to his dream becomes lost and unidentifiable, and his spiritual resources have been lessened, and the loss of meaning in existence has grown, why should he resign himself to such an art?

There is no implication of a call to arms or a desire to smite any villain hip and thigh. We cannot tell the artist what to do. We cannot apply prohibitions and sanctions. This is not a collectivized state where art, too, must be devoted to serving the state in some form of sweetness and light. There is no need for still another academy, left or right.

But faced with a brutal dehumanization of art, a feeling of outrage is unavoidable. Such a feeling is rooted in the instinct for survival which cannot accept the diminishment of man as inexorable, even though he is under attack from every quarter. Art need not be an instrument of alienation. There are enough other such instruments around us. This last seems the unkindest cut of all. A basis for mutuality is essential. Art and man are parting at an increasing rate and both will suffer for it, but the public can do little about it. The public cannot serve as a critic. It is not equipped for the task. It is the public in the end which makes the final judgment, but such judgment needs time and understanding. The public has little basis for choice now.

In order to make a choice, one must understand. It is difficult to understand today when each new departure is proclaimed the ultimate demonstration of truth and integrity, though the evidence is shrouded in obscure metaphysical terms and ontologies. What follows is a brief look at several art forms, the qualities inherent in them, the forces working on them, and the esthetic development which led to their present state. The commentaries upon the events and qualities unavoidably are opinions which stem from the belief that art needs man, for it is verging on the absurd with its endless contemplation of its own navel. The technical tricks are running out. Originality has descended to novelty, and meaning and nobility have given way to fashion.

Man needs art. He is adrift in an increasingly incomprehensible world. He must retain every spiritual resource possible.

A basis for mutuality perhaps can be re-established by the recognition of the processes and motivations that have caused the artist to turn his back on man. If these can be understood with sympathy and the importance of mutuality be acknowledged, then art, now armed with new power and freedom of expression, can again become a spiritual bulwark for man; and man, his understanding and sensitivity enlarged, again can provide the artist with the ultimate motivation.

Esthetics and Originality

First Phase, 1830–1914

There's a combative artist named Whistler
Who is like his own hog hairs, a bristler.
   A tube of white lead
   and a punch on the head
Offer varied attractions to Whistler.

So went the limerick by Dante Gabriel Rossetti. His subject was, of course, that dashing butterfly armed with a sting, James Abbott McNeill Whistler. Its intention was a two-edged criticism, a comment on Whistler's painting "The White Girl" and on Whistler's vaunted reputation for pugnacity (he had just pushed his stuffy brother-in-law through a plate-glass window in Paris). The time was the 1860s and the limerick sums up the double-barreled distaste held by the art establishment then current for the avant-gardists of the day.

Newness was in ferment and young originals were

beginning to shoulder aside the high priests of the art of taste establishment. The areas of contention were concerned with not only the rejection of odd esthetic ideas, but odd personal behavior as well. By 1860 the revolution in art had been in full career for several decades and originality had come to be associated with strange attitudes, dress and behavior as well as with new ideas. The prickly prophets of the new did not settle for wearing their beliefs as brassards on their arms. They were engrossed in their beliefs and carried them into every area of living.

In this day we have come to accept the idea of the artist as a man totally different from the commuting, bill-paying sons of Adam. It is taken for granted, of course, that he is a man of greater sensitivity and sensibility—a man who can articulate and illuminate emotions which are buried under the surface of consciousness and can magically spur the sense of recognition. Because the artist, through his genius, or at worst, talent, is the agency that helps us discover hidden sources of beauty and emotions, we are willing to set him up as a member of a priestly sect involved with our lives, but yet outside the everyday business of living. This sense of difference has existed for ages.

But the idea of the artist as a man who flaunts his individuality and separation from society, not necessarily as an accident of his personality but rather as one who conducts himself in a manner likely to be a flagrant affront to every reasonable concept of behavior, as a badge of his trade, is a relatively new idea. In the centuries-long history of art, this acceptance of the artist as a nonparticipating member in society is a recent innovation; yet the idea has attained great credence and acceptance with short-term benefits to the artist and less to other men. The feverish drive for the kind of originality in existence today started a little more than one hundred years ago—a little more than a man's lifetime, but an instant of time in the history of art. It is the overwhelming motivation impelling art today.

By 1860 the drive for originality in idea and behavior had reached noteworthy levels. Never before had there been such a difference between the artist and the rest of society. Originality had always been a precious ingredient in art, although the degree of permissible departure from a norm was largely dependent upon the demands and strictures laid by society upon artists for each given period. Thus, during the priest-ridden Egyptian and Byzantine periods, the artist was a craftsman within the framework of his society and rarely known. In Greek antiquity the artist worked within a strict discipline and he, too, was anonymous. It was in the richly humanist, later classical period that a few sculptors emerged. Most of the painters of that period still are anonymous. Before the Renaissance, recognition in the arts seems to have been extended mostly to writers.

In Greek art of antiquity, during the Mycenaean and Minoan periods in the first millennium B.C., the discipline of form and even of subject was strict, and the artist little known. In the period that followed, until about 400 B.C., the early archaic, we find the disciplines still hold, although the form is enriched.

The subject matter that will persist for centuries begins to appear. The heroes Agamemnon, Menelaus and Achilles stand and fight on the sides of vases and cups. Relatively little is known of architects and sculptors, although the names of some cup painters such as Euphronios, Exekias and Duris have come down.

In the richly humanist fifth century B.C. the Greeks produced an art of extraordinary beauty within a framework of exact discipline. Again, little is known of painters and architects. It is the writers' and sculptors' turn to emerge from the darkness of time. Although even in the case of Pheidias, the sculptor generally considered the greatest of the period, we know him by reputation through copies of his work. No work is certain to be from his hand. We know the names of Myron and Polyclitus through some of their works and through copies. In the same way we know Praxiteles, the sculptor of the fourth century B.C.

During the medieval and Gothic periods, the church was the single great organization to remain strong in spiritual and temporal power. The art of the period was concentrated largely around the Christian religion and its dominant organizations.

By and large, the Renaissance saw the artist break out of the medieval and Gothic constrictions to re-explore classical ideals and enlarge them. Innovation, bursting with imagination and vigor, came in a great outpouring despite the disciplines which were created to contain them. Its effects were so overpowering as to halt major new developments for several centuries.

It probably took that long to digest what had been swallowed whole. It was at this time that the artist emerged from total or partial anonymity and was an individual with his own identity.

In all these periods, however, one paramount relationship was consistent: namely, the artist was an integrated member of society. He was an artisan, craftsman and worker of elevated skills within the social structure. He associated with his fellow men, wearing the same dress and conducting himself in the same manner. He was a member of the community. While he was still a member of the community, in the centuries from the Renaissance up until the French Revolution, the status of the artist had been undergoing change. This was nowhere so marked as in the relationship between the artist and his patron or his lack of patron. This condition began to affect his relationship with his society. The great and extraordinary change for the artist came with the destruction of the old order in Europe—the eruption of Napoleon, the introduction of new societies and egalitarian ideas which brought with them the promise of a new kind of life.

The Napoleonic Wars had spread a tide of blood and of ideas across the face of Europe. When they were over only despair and disillusion were left. Nowhere was this so true as in France. France had been bled white: first by the guillotine, then by *la Gloire*. The promised ideals for which all this blood had been spilt was an empty dream. The patrons of the ancient regime were gone. The brilliance of the upper bourgeoisie had lost its shine. All that was left were the survivors—money-grubbing, middle-class peasants, and small merchants. The artist living in this disillusioned aftermath of Napoleon found little sympathy and less support. He therefore became defiant and opposed to society at nearly every point where their lives met. If the society was moral, the artist became a proponent of amorality. If there was a conservative ideal of law and order, the artist associated himself with anarchistic ideas. If the main body of society was devoted to money-grubbing, the artist showed his contempt by his disdain for money. The fellowship of such opposition banded the artists into a group who were devoted to a studied offense against the proprieties of a bourgeois society.

Such was the start of the artist as a professional nonconformist. To this day the appellation "Bohemian" is carried by artists, an inheritance from the days when the artists inhabited a hazy, imaginary place which had no geographical identity. This no-place, more a state of mind than a district, was where artists, painters, writers and musicians joined in ideas and opposition to the society from which they disassociated themselves, a society toward which they felt little sense of obligation.

The ideals, joys and tragedies of that day were recorded in Henri Murger's *Scènes de la vie de Bohème*. The effect of this book is still with us, since it was the source of the libretto for Puccini's *La Bohème,* a most charming and popular opera. To this day, therefore, through that opera we are still made conscious of the attitude of those Bohemians. The heroes are defiant and ineffective dreamers. Villains are rich and idiotic. The women, docile and beautiful houris, are at hand for the willful pleasures of the artists. Money is to be despised and sought only for the unfortunate necessity of providing food, drink and shelter, and then secured only by chicanery, wit and cunning.

But despite the poverty and personal tragedy, it was a blessed nirvana, bathed in an aura of a gay, carefree, casual approach to life, which was given its purpose and direction by dedication to art. With such a sense of apartness, bolstered by a jointly held dedication, a feeling of caste developed. Since they were artists and therefore felt superior, and because they despised the bourgeois society, these artists, as typified by Murger's heroes, Rodolphe, Marcel, Schaunard, came to assume the mantle of an aristocracy of the mind and spirit. The bond of dedication to an ideal, the assumption of an attitude of aristocratic superiority, solidified the feeling of a separate caste. When to all this was added the external clan symbols of flamboyance, strange personal behavior and dress, the chasm between the artist and society was made clear.

Separation received an added impetus from artists who, while not impoverished, were creating situations and beliefs calculated to fan even more the flames of antagonism between a bourgeois society and rebellious artists. Two men had a remarkable impact upon the fledgling new art consciousness, its effects felt to this day. They were the flamboyant Théophile Gautier, author of that pagan paean to amorality, *Mademoiselle de Maupin,* and the intense poet and critic Charles Baudelaire. From them came a slogan credited to Gautier. It was that great tocsin and clarion, "art for

art's sake." The crystallization of this position grew
out of many discussions of esthetics.

Esthetics was not a new philosophic discovery. The
nature of beauty had been examined by Plato and
Aristotle, by the Renaissance humanists, and finally
codified and systematized by the Germans, who, in
their adoration of systems, sought to reduce the nature
of beauty to a scientific theorem of esthetics. Immanuel
Kant defined esthetics as "the science which treats
the condition of sensuous perception." His fellow
Teutons Hegel and Schopenhauer added their pro-
fundities to the labyrinthine structure of words and
ideas. Esthetics had become a brand-new world of
thought staked out by the Germans.

But now it was miraculously turned into an activist
war cry. Fresh and adventurous, it became the launch-
ing platform for inspiration. The new men were not
satisfied with the accepted tenets of beauty. They
sought it everywhere. At the root of their search was
still a relentless desire for separation from the smug-
ness of a middle-class society. Even ugliness and degradation were not unbeautiful as long as they were
not the sort of things identified with a despised society.

This rejection of normally accepted standards was
going on in England as well as in France. In England
it occurred in isolated instances, rather than as a wide-
scale movement. De Quincey and Coleridge delved
into art divorced from morality. De Quincey went as
far as to explore his addiction to opium as a source
of art. He had considerable influence upon Baudelaire,
whose own indulgence in sensuality and vice had
moved him to the same extenuation of sensation while

curiously assuming the air and costume of a severely sober Englishman. Baudelaire was a strange amalgam of severity of mien and manners while indulging himself in exotic sensual relationships with a Negro mistress and associations with sexual deviates. All of his experience heightened his sensitivity to strange ideals of beauty which he finally summed up in his *Les Fleurs du mal*.

These, then, were the multiple influences which helped develop a posture for the artist. He was at odds with the mainstream of society in ideals, behavior and manners. He was given a splendid organizing device in the slogan succinctly stated as "art for art's sake" and clearly defined by declarations such as Baudelaire's "Poetry has no other end but itself; it cannot have any other." And by attacking the very basis of a law-abiding society through means as extraordinary as the elevation of vice and degradation as a source for beauty in art, the separation of the artist from other men was well established.

This was a beginning—it still goes on. The decadence first explored by De Quincey and Baudelaire was made into an act of self-immolation by those strange lovers, the poets Verlaine and Rimbaud; into a way of life by the English poets Ernest Dowson, James Thomson and Francis Thompson. The tradition continues today through those who still believe in regeneration through degradation. We have examples in the life, times and attitudes of William Burroughs as reported in his book *Naked Lunch*. We see it staring out at us from slick magazines in interviews with such dedicated destroyers of middle-class morality as Allen Ginsberg, author of the poem "Howl."

Clustered in coffee houses in New York and San Francisco can be found the amorphous groups who are called the beatniks. They exist as a group, with few if any individual identities established. Their main pursuit seems to be protest, in the course of which they compulsively champion *outré* causes and hep art forms. Their clan badges of honor are Bohemian attire, off-beat manners and loudly proclaimed, if not practiced, acts of social protest such as addiction to the hep narcotics of "pot" and "horse." Their major impact on the arts so far, it seems, is to provide magazines such as *The New Yorker* and *Esquire* with cartoon material. But underneath all of this outlandish surface is an underlying philosophical despairing reaction to our society, as developed in Sartre's version of existentialism.

But decadence or separation, as an act in itself, was not the only outcome of this early drive for originality. When shackles are broken, great strides forward can be made in the resulting freedoms, not as a conscious decision but as a natural concomitant. And so, when it was apparent to a few artists that the idea of freedom was in itself not the desideratum, a group of serious-minded workers thoughtfully and ardently developed new concepts for their art. They were able to convert the questioning of the artistic dogma of an accepted order into a purposeful, deliberate and disciplined search for new forms and solutions. Their talk was not so much of rebellion as it was a professional and thoughtful examination of ideas. The group who made up this company are known to us now as the impressionists. At the root of their adventure into form and color was a theoretical or ideological base. In other areas of social behavior they were quiet— Monet, Pissarro, Sisley, their fellow impressionists as well as their forerunners, the seminal artists such as Courbet, Manet and Degas. They did not use up their energies in outrageous personal display. The points of conflict with the public were not concerned with dress or manner. For that matter, there was little contact with the public. The conflicts were with the art establishment—those who dominated the salons and the critical journalists. The very name "impressionist" was first used as a term of opprobrium by a journalist. Monet had explained a picture as an impression. *Le Charivari* sloughed off all such painters as impressionists. It has now become a glorious title.

There was really only one scandalous incident. Manet had painted a genre studio picture of two soberly clothed young men calmly seated in a woodland glade, paying scant attention to a nude, nubile female companion. She is staring out of the picture, quite unconcerned with her state of undress in the company of her heavily clothed companions. A second young female, clutching a diaphanous shift to her breasts, clambers out of a stream. The painting, "Le dejeuner sur l'herbe," had a classical ancestor in Giorgione's "Concert Champêtre." If Manet had undressed everybody and given them pagan names, the painting would have passed off without a stir. But the one *nude poule* was too much. All of the imagined licentiousness and lubricity of the artists, pent up in middle-class minds so long, was aroused and the storm was on. Turned down by the salon, the picture was exhibited at the Salon des Refusés. It was an occasion for the bourgeois to burn witches. They marched through the rebels' salon hissing at and booing the exhibits.

But except for this isolated instance, the painters were permitted to grow up in peace. Occasionally there would be a journalistic explosion. *Le Figaro* held that painting had fallen into such low estate that all you had to do to be a painter was to throw color haphazardly on canvas and then sign it. (Today, when this method of painting is an actuality under the title of action painting, a newspaper critic making a pejorative comment does so with the fear of standing accused first of a lack of understanding, and second of being a Philistine. It no longer is comfortable to wear the robe of a Philistine. For that matter, it really is difficult to find one. They have all taken to the hills.)

In Paris the exciting and original ideas spread out and students came from all over to learn and drink deep of the heady discoveries. From England came a group of very English acolytes and an American. They were blessed with enthusiasm and substantial incomes. Something grand has gone out of living when men settle for simple names. These men had names full of orotund sound, worthy of governors of the Bank of England or at the very least prime ministers. There was George Louis Palmella Busson du Maurier, who was to write *Trilby*. You can imagine the ideas which this book engendered. The title was borrowed to label a brand of Dr. Condom's ingenious sheaths, probably a more significant recognition than to borrow a name for a sleeping car.

Then there was Edward John Poynter, a future president of the Royal Academy. And certainly there was James Abbott McNeill Whistler, the anglicized American. There were others, but their names are too short to mention. The English invasion carried along its British phlegm and its addiction to muscular regeneration if not the esthetic dedication. Mornings were spent in the atelier Gleyre, building up mind and spirit; afternoons in their studios, where in addition to painting they spent time building up their bodies by boxing, fencing, swinging Indian clubs, and by all manner of activities which have been part of English upper-class birthrights from the playing fields of Eton on. Evenings they ate in restaurants that could provide good basic staples like roast beef and mutton. Such were the student days of a prominent group of Englishmen in Paris at the time.

But not so Whistler. He took to Paris like a duck to water. Exercise he thought to be fit work for a concierge and he developed a palate for food, color and behavior. When the Englishmen went home, they did not carry back much of the art, but they did carry back the ferment in the world of art. All were reabsorbed into English life; all, that is, but Whistler, who brought not only the spirit of French art, but two French artists as well. One Frenchman, eventually to be famous, and certainly not to be outdone in the matter of names, was Ignace Henri Jean Théodore Fantin-Latour.

Once returned, Whistler fobbed off his friends on his long-suffering brother-in-law and went about building a reputation for himself. He found an art-conscious country. The middle-class was buying pictures and the artists were reaping a rich reward. British artists were exotic and original, too, but not in the gusty manner of the inhabitants of Bohemia. They were rarefied, rich and upper-class by association rather than by assumption. The pre-Raphaelites were dominant. Rossetti, William Morris and Edward Burne-Jones were infusing England with an image of a romantic ancient past. Behavior and dress followed the same sort of idyllic romantic pattern. Rossetti had a private menagerie replete with peacocks. Dandyism, a mark of the *bon ton* since the regency, still flourished. Whistler, always a dandy, now became a veritable Beau Brummel, equipped with a long wandlike walking stick, which he used to punch periods onto his quips, and a monocle through which he stared in disbelief at the fatuous world around him. A whole era of upper-class bad manners, disguised behind epigrams and faultless tailoring, was ushered in. What esthetes lacked in originality of thought they made up for in originality of behavior.

Other artists swung cudgels against conformity. Algernon Charles Swinburne was in a tearing sweat of creativity and of dissipation. He assiduously applied himself to a revolt against Victorian orthodoxy. He was expelled from the Arts Club because he played hopscotch on the somber tall black silk hats of members gathered in solemn conclave. He admired Baudelaire and wrote poems in imitation and in praise. He longed to be evil and pretended to the curious indulgences advocated by the Marquis de Sade but for which he had neither the stomach nor the physique. But in his writings he conjured up mysterious "new passion for daytime and night" and had everyone wondering how awful or delicious the sins "seventy times seven" really were. The esthetes were titillated by the suggestions of strange sensual delights of vice and indulgence as indicated in "Rococo" from *Poems and Ballads*.

We have heard from hidden places
What love scarce lives and hears:
We have seen on fervent faces
The pallor of strange tears:

Every other stanza of this poem ends with the relationship of pleasure and pain, the antiphonal delights of the "divine marquis":

Nor crush the lees of pleasure
From sanguine grapes of pain.

And:

A single sob of pleasure,
A single pulse of pain.

And:

Foams round the feet of pleasure
The blood-red must of pain.

And:

And earlier leaf of pleasure,
And latter flower of pain.

So, starting in the elegant drawing rooms of London and in university quadrangles, a strange brand of estheticism was let loose on the land. Vice to some was an unsought basis of undoing. So it was for Oscar Fingal O'Flahertie Wills (ring out the names) Wilde. Wilde, a brilliant Irishman fresh from Oxford and the influence of John Ruskin and Walter Pater, came to London bound to make his mark. He went where the action was and thrust himself on Whistler and Swinburne, who were so overwhelmed by his push and audacity that they accepted him. Calling himself a professor of esthetics, and clothing himself in a rarefied air and a preposterous costume said to be copied from a du Maurier drawing in *Punch,* he sallied forth. Wearing velvet knickerbockers, velvet jacket edged with black braid, silk stockings, patent leather pumps, a Byronic shirt and flowing tie, he brought "cultcha" to the Philistines.

In spite of his dress, or perhaps because of it, he was a success, much to the annoyance of those he was purporting to help. An original in behavior and thought, he finally fell afoul of the law for his sexual tastes, and he was tried and incarcerated for the despoiling of the young Lord Alfred Douglas; and with that the career of an activator in the cult of "art for art's sake" came to a dreary end.

There were many more of such upper-class estheticians. Noteworthy were George Moore and Aubrey Beardsley, whose contributions to originality of work were in a narrow stylistic range but much broader in the impact and impression of their attitude of personal behavior. By their success and acceptance they set a pattern for subsequent times, a pattern that has been adapted and used by many esthetic adventurers to help them make a mark on the world when other forms of inspiration seem hopeless.

While these precious high jinks were going on in England, artists in France were still passionately involved in ideological experiments and developments which flowered into magnificent new conceptions of painting art. The post-impressionists, many of whom started as Bohemians, attained the position of respected masters in their own lifetimes. Such was the case just in time for Cézanne, while unhappily not as true for Gauguin and Van Gogh, whose fame and high earning capacity came too late for them to relish it. But at the same time that the quiet discoveries were going on, there was a host of less self-effacing artists and esthetes who still remained completely dedicated to the idea of the ever-new, the strange and original. This aim still had its central motivation in the desire to shock the middle class and by bringing attention to themselves, to achieve their individual identity. The technical and ideological discoveries were beginning to set the knowing world on its ear. Originality was a heady experience. Nothing was yet codified or established; there still were fortresses of smug acceptance to storm. The world of art was bright and young. Bright and young though it was, the brothel painters Toulouse-Lautrec and, later, Jules Pascin used bourgeois sex and absinthe drinking as jaundiced comments upon society and subjects with which to develop individual styles and techniques.

This irrepressible spirit and complete freedom pushed others on to the verge of anti-art. A famous hoax near the turn of the century was perpetrated when a group of young artists led by Dorgeles, an author, created a picture painted by the tail of the donkey pet of the owner of the Café Lapin Agile. The work, impressionist in style, was hung in the Salon des Indépendants. Gorgeously titled "And the sun went down over the Adriatic," it was signed by Joachim Raphael Boronali. The painting received a good deal of praise. We do not make the same kind of mistake today. When an ape paints a picture the truth is not hidden. When the simian esthete in the Cincinnati zoo completes a work, the picture is clearly labeled "Ape Painting." But it is bought in any case. Who knows, maybe some day the ape will be famous.

A tightrope was being walked between buffoonery and artistic ideation. The artists who surrounded and followed the great masters of contemporary painting were filled with a macabre, dedicated frivolity. In apologia they said that Degas and Manet lived in a time when it was not necessary to be part of the absurdities upon which they commented.

The business of antic behavior in company with advanced esthetics was not limited to painters. Originality verging on the absurd was the hallmark of the career and works of the composer Erik Satie. Satie is chiefly remembered for his extravagant Bohemianism and his compositions in a sort of musical cabalese. His work is occasionally exhumed to get a little extra mileage out of shock value. September of 1963 saw a performance of a Satie composition in New York. A dozen new avant-gardists played Satie's *Vexations* to a veritably empty house for 18 hours and 40 minutes. The work was for piano and consisted of 180 notes. The composer's instructions called for it to be repeated 840 times.

Harold Schonberg in *The New York Times* the next day plaintively wondered, "Why 840? It could just as easily have been 1,000 or 329." But there is no one around to supply the answer. Eight hundred and forty is a good round number, and why not? If you are dedicated, you do what the composer says. Anyway, it was a gasser.

Though Satie mostly is remembered as an eccentric, he was a friend and guide to both Debussy and Ravel. He delighted in outrageously strange titles as well as his instructions. There are titles like "Trois Morceaux en forme de poire," "Descriptions automatiques," "Gnossiennes," "Trois Préludes flasques (pour un chien)." He was sarcastic and irascible—endearing qualities he carried to his audience, for whom he always had the lowest regard. From his workaday living of playing in night haunts and whorehouses he, in company with other kindred souls, would make an occasional foray against an audience and then retire again. Satie was representative of one kind of considered affront to the normalcy of his society.

Just as a musician found it necessary to place himself at odds with his community, so did a writer. He was that picaresque Bohemian, Alfred Henri Jarry, another man driven by the urgency to shock and to divorce himself from ordinary society as a basis for his esthetics. A friend once described him as being "too original for his own good, lacking the balance which prevents some people from always putting the cart before the horse." Jarry made a fetish out of originality, from meals, which he ate backwards from dessert to soup, to wearing an odd assortment of clothes. He normally dressed like a bicycle racer but he sported evening costumes consisting of a white canvas suit with a paper shirt upon which he painted a tie. In his later years he even began to lose his identity to one of his original creations. He had created a character named King Ubu and a language and a set of attitudes that went with him. Jarry constantly quoted his king as a source, so that he eventually came to be known as Père Ubu. Drink and dissipation turned Jarry's life into a long-drawn-out suicidal frenzy. His life merged with his creation and it no longer was clear who was doing the writing, Jarry or Ubu; whether the alter ego was dictating, or whether Jarry was still in control.

He delighted in demeaning most of man's sacred institutions. "Love is an act of no importance; it can be repeated indefinitely," said he in *Messaline*. While he was not an important creator who left an indelible mark, he had considerable influence upon the new young men who were in quest of their own identity. In creating an atmosphere of unreality he was a surrealist before the name was given to a school. He provided a rallying point and a focus for the high priests of surrealism-to-be: André Breton, Max Jacob, André Salomon and Guillaume Apollinaire.

The latter was another esthete who found it necessary to intensify the separation between middle-class and esthetic ideals—different from Jarry, but like him in his ability to affect those around him. He was not responsible for works of notable importance, but rather was the great art impressario of his time; not an artist to the public, but an artist to artists. He was the *chef d'école* of the painting school of Paris without being a painter. A lover of Marie Laurencin, a founder of numerous reviews, he even had the dramatic experience of being jailed as a suspect in the theft of the "Mona Lisa" from the Louvre. He was a great proponent of ideas current in a time of frenzied creativity.

Born Guillaume Albert Wladimir Alexandre Apollinaire de Kostrowitski (what splendid sounds!), the illegitimate son of a demimondaine in Rome, he came to Paris from the Riviera, where he spent his youth, and plunged immediately into the bubbling caldron of new art faiths. His friendships with Picasso, Braque, Jacob, Salomon, Vlaminck and Derain put him in the vortex of ideas. With all his dedicated avant-gardism, he was practical in his day-to-day conduct. He visited his mother weekly for a square meal and like a modern schoolboy took along a bag of dirty laundry to be washed. He kept his head just above poverty by producing a flood of prose and poetry for esthetes, and of pornography for more rarefied consumption. But his major force and contribution were as articulator and broadcaster of the many-sided ideas of his time.

It was a time of great discovery and experiment. African art, the final flaunting of middle-class niceties, powerful, aboriginal, ugly-beautiful in its primacy and passion, burst onto the scene. Picasso painted his portentous "Les Demoiselles d'Avignon"; Modigliani painted his gentle portraits and nudes in the first reactions to this primitive culture. And then, out of Cézanne's last geometric studies of nature, came cubism. Picasso, Braque, Picabia, Gris, all helped bring it into being, a great flood that carried everything before it.

With the abandonment of the last vestiges of representation, avant-garde originality was no longer the mark of the eccentric. It had become the order of the day. The last years before World War I saw an incredible eruption. Artists were striking out in every direction; style after style tumbled into being. It was almost as though the war had been ordained by some superconsciousness in order to call a halt to new ideas and give time to sort them out. Cubism, orphism in France, futurism in France and Italy, vorticism in England, rayonism, suprematism and constructivism in Russia, expressionism in Germany, all happened within a short space of time.

Joyce was becoming known. So was D. H. Lawrence. Debussy and Ravel had written their ballets for Diaghilev and Stravinsky his *Le Sacre du printemps* for the same company. Schönberg was beginning his experiments with the 12-tone scale. In America modern art arrived in one big bang—the Armory Show—which created a great stir. The world was filled with originality rampant.

From the disillusionment in the aftermath of the Napoleonic Wars and the abortive revolution of 1848 had come an inspired spirit of defiance. A great revolutionary movement, with the artists in rebellion against the world around them, had been set in motion, a revolution which had brought about a remarkable regeneration and re-energizing of art. Despite, or perhaps through, the oddities and exotica, a great esthetic realization had come about, still leaving bright avenues for further exploration. But hand in hand with the accomplishment had come a polarized attitude of rejection of society and it institutions, the acceptance of the idea that the artist and society were separate and inimical.

Such a concept carried with it the seeds of anti-humanism and eventually of anti-art. It contained the guarantee of a continuance and extension of separation of man and art. Such was the nature of the first phase of the esthetic revolution. It ended with the First World War.

Esthetics and Originality

Second Phase, 1914–

If disillusionment was the distillation of the Napoleonic aftermath, then disgust was the essence of the reaction to World War I. Disgust with a torn and ruptured world and with all of its institutions which made such a bloodletting possible. The artist's old adversary, the middle class, was broadened to include all of its social institutions, and the attacks on orthodoxy were not launched as a single dashing foray, but were made across a broad front, and as a considered and constant attitude.

The impact of the war on art was very deep. Yet social man has enormous recuperative powers. His instinct is to cover scars and wounds of a disturbed order as well as he can, and he attempts to re-establish as rapidly as possible his own comfortable norm. But art, the creation of man, seems to adapt itself at a different pace. Originality and newness normally energize it toward change. When these have been accelerated and the direction of art has been changed in its motivation, then, like molecules rearranging themselves in a new physical relationship, it is difficult, even impossible, to arrest the continuous process of change along the new course. So, the effect of the war on art was to end the esthetic developments in Germany and Russia. Individual artists were torn loose from their moorings, physically and psychologically, and thrust into geographical and spiritual exile. One aspect of this reaction of disgust took the form of an anti-art movement called Dada.

Dada developed during the war in two cities which were not directly in the path of war-making—New York and Zurich. In New York City its principal proponents were the painters Marcel Duchamp, Francis Picabia and Man Ray. In Switzerland they were the painter-sculptor Hans Arp and the poet Tristan Tzara. After the war the movement appeared in Germany, where Kurt Schwitters and Max Ernst were moving forces. It eventually came to Paris, where it was first given vociferous espousal by André Breton and Louis Aragon, later aided by Paul Eluard and Tristan Tzara. It gradually metamorphosed into other forms.

The work of the movement was marked by irreverence for established norms and by irrationality, displayed in the assemblage of materials, forms and symbols which had no natural relationship one to the other or any counterpart in the natural world. Chiefly, it attempted to demonstrate the absurdities of living. The basic urge was anarchical. Scandals were to be sought rather than avoided. A capsule career of Duchamp provides a summation of the underlying disdain for esthetic attitudes in art and for art audiences which was characteristic of Dada. Irreverence for the art of the past, as when Duchamp pasted a mustache on a reproduction of the "Mona Lisa" and exhibited it with resulting international repercussions. Disrespect for the materials of his craft, as when he painted several large pictures on glass which cracked during transport, at which time he declared that since that had been his original intention, he considered the pictures ready for viewing. And at last, his final act of disdain for art itself, for he gave it up to devote the rest of his days to chess.

The core of the intention of Dada was absurdity— the artists' comment on modern life and esthetics. The techniques employed were equally strange. Collage, with which brief experiments had been made by the artists in their search for textural innovation before the war, was now pushed to realize the potential which lay in irrational relationships.

Dada became an organized movement in Zurich during 1916. Several anarchic painters and poets founded a group with headquarters at a place called Cabaret Voltaire. The movement did not come by its name for any generic reason, but rather was given a name by an arbitrary choice from the Larousse dictionary meaning "hobby horse"; it had a sufficiently nonsensical ring. The Cabaret Voltaire, an ancestor of the present-day "beat" coffee houses, witnessed a startling series of highly original innovations. Weird dances and charades, perhaps not unlike the contemporary versions called "happenings," were performed. Junk music of accidental sounds, poems of nonsense, of simultaneous declamation in several languages or of imaginary languages, were offered. These exotic exercises were interlarded with occasional serious readings and lectures.

Dada as a movement ran out in the '20s, although a few individual artists clung to their individual versions and techniques, adapting themselves as well as they could to the newer innovations which were emerging. Though the movement came to an end, its anti-estheticism never was entirely lost and appears even today in versions called pop art in painting and assemblage in sculpture.

Paris had become the Mecca of originality and creativity. Painters, sculptors and writers all poured into the city of light and esthetic experimentation. From England, Ireland, but mainly from the United States, a group of writers had come to escape the narrow, middle-class mediocrity and biased orthodoxy of their homelands. They came to experience the cultural freedom and the atmosphere of explosive creativity which marked the artistic life of Paris. Some were great and original creators; others accurate reporters who summed up an era with artistry and candor. Still others were catalysts, not responsible themselves for works of lasting significance, but who by their experiments, friendship and aid to fellow artists helped bring an extraordinary burst of creativity into being within a compressed period of time. Nearly every shade of contemporary writing was represented, not constrained to a school. There were those who dwelt heavily on the textural quality and symbolism of words. They made heavy demands upon the sensitivity and erudition of their readers. There were writers who conveyed a sense of realism with hammer-blow intensity and still others who tore from writing all polite convention, using situations, images, words and descriptions normally associated with pornography, but here used with the intention of stripping from an artificial world all pretension disguised behind an artificial use of words. Freud, Marx and the new esthetic posture all had consequent impact on the ideas current. They came out either as ferocious indictments or in the gentler tone of calm despair.

The writers, most of whom knew one another and at one time or another exchanged ideas which helped bring about this extraordinary and explosive creative outburst, read like a *Who's Who* of modern letters. In Paris in that decade were James Joyce, Ezra Pound, Ernest Hemingway, Robert McAlmon, Gertrude Stein, Archibald MacLeish, F. Scott Fitzgerald, Thornton Wilder, E. E. Cummings, Katherine Anne Porter and Henry Miller. T. S. Eliot and Stephen Vincent Benét would come to visit, exchange ideas, hear and learn. The list is seemingly endless.

But in the striking out with new ideas of style and of content, a new and far-reaching element was introduced. The use of words for their textural effect, rather than for their communicative values, introduced a level of self-conscious obscurantism which, extended today, has in some cases reached the level of utter nonsense. This period introduced the idea of a reduced level of communicative transference and the concept of the use of words for their tonal and emotional effect whether they were understood or not. It was an important entering wedge in the cleavage between avant-garde writing and the common man and sowed seeds for future alienations. It also became important, through Freudian ideals, to free oneself from inhibitions and to free one's libido. In some writings, the use of sex in the context of the work, scatological references and descriptions of scenes verged on the obscene and pornographic, if in fact they were not so. Once the intention is recognized, it is possible to accept the fornications so lovingly described as a sublimated declaration of independence from Grundyism and a desire to reach a stripped-bare realism.

There were great changes taking place in the painters' world as well. Beyond the effect of the war in the stimulation of an art of skepticism and absurdity, as in Dada, art was due for a great reversal. There was bound to be a normal reaction to the uncompromisingly dogmatic beliefs extant just before the war; even without the advent of the war this must have happened.

Painting had been dominated by strong ideological theories. From the impressionists through Cézanne and the analytical cubists, painters had been motivated by a desire to organize their work into new systems built around theories of form and color. It was inevitable that a reaction to this kind of intellectual control would set in. All movements are impelled to a great degree by cyclical action and reaction. In the need to be original, it is implicit that what has come immediately before must be abandoned if not annihilated. In recent years, with the pace of change increased, the pendulum swings of style come close, one on the heels of another. Action painting was relatively short-lived; pop art, almost its direct antithesis, is following closely on.

In this decade we can see this happening in architecture as well. Even while the older masters are still working in the strict geometric linearity of vertical, horizontal relationships, all surfaces reflecting the smooth finish of the machine, the younger architects have gone to the other extreme. They are creating curvilinear shapes in rough concrete, destroying what is left of the surface with hammers to create roughened and accidental texture, the antithesis of machine surfaces. This kind of reaction has marked the zigzag progress of art, each generation impelled to react strongly against the preceding. In the past, established styles often were so dominant that it was difficult to escape for several generations. Today the life of a style is shorter. The taste for novelty has overcome former bases for value judgment. The desire for novelty infects not only the art buyer, but the artist himself, so that he can manage to find ways to accommodate his integrity to shifting fashion. Some men, impelled by the force of changing styles, will change their styles several times within their own lifetime. Some men remain secure in their own inner vision. They move serenely on, relatively untroubled by what is going on around them. Two such men working in architecture today are Italy's Luigi Nervi and Mexico's Felix Candella. While it is unquestionably true that they have been working within a relatively restricted grammar of form and problem, nevertheless there is a consistent structural poetry in their work without the sense of straining for effect. However, by and large it is the instinct of the artist to destroy what came before. How else can an identity for an individual be created?

And so it was for the artists in the period after World War I. In response to such an underlying inevitability and with the recent experience of Dada as a catalyst, a new movement arose. It was the early formative stages of a movement later to be called surrealism. While employing resemblances in technique to Picasso, Picabia and Braque, it was a new approach to form. Still reacting to the moral breakdown and financial disarray of the postwar period, it carried over the desire to destroy all of the accepted norms, especially those in painting. The Catalan Joan Miró, an early leader of the movement, said: "I want to assassinate painting."

The central doctrine of the art was to liberate the unconscious into extra-pictorial expressions. It was a form of automatism, obeying the subconscious mind, with a minimal control by reason, using any graphic means which came to hand. The work naturally was extremely individualistic and not organized into a school, since few stylistic ordinates existed.

Miró, Klee and Masson demonstrate the individual approach. Miró's work reflects ingenuity, spontaneity and a search for the essense of a symbol or sign. Masson's work was mystical, his subject matter haunted by an intensely private set of symbols which had come to have universal meaning for him, his form full of arabesques and curving rhythm. Klee's work is a magnificent realization of form, poetry and evocation. It contains the paradoxical elements of ideational simplicity in complex relationships, all held together by a rational order of form.

These three represent one aspect of surrealism or as some have called it, "fantacism," in that they used flat surfaces with no modeling in a two-dimensional picture plane. There are, however, three painters who are more immediately thought of as most representative of surrealism. They are Yves Tanguy, Max Ernst and Salvador Dali.

Max Ernst is the surrealist's surrealist, although in this country Salvador Dali's work has come to be the hallmark of the school. Ernst wanders in and out of schools of painting, but always carries with him his private visions. He uses collage and frottage, a system of rubbing over wood, plaster or cloth, the results of which he uses as a basis for a painting or a drawing. The images which accidentally emerge suggest pictures to his subconscious. His is a deliberate search for a method of inducing a subconscious image.

Yves Tanguy is said to have taken up painting after seeing one of Giorgio di Chirico's works, and the influence is evident. Where di Chirico used an approximation of natural objects, some real and some contrived, in three-dimensional space to achieve a haunting, mystical quality, Tanguy uses amorphous forms arranged in three-dimensional space. While lacking the immediacy that comes from recognition, existing in the di Chiricos, the Tanguy paintings convey a remote feeling of the unknown by somewhat like means.

Surrealism has dead-ended more or less in recent years with Salvador Dali. It cannot be said whether the ghost will be forever laid or whether it will reappear. Painters are still working in that direction. However, for the time being it is not the painting of the moment. Dali shows influences from many sources —the atmosphere of di Chirico and Tanguy and the techniques of the baroque. His subjects are dreams and hallucinations with highly Freudian overtones. Since his subject matter required para-realism in some unusual relationship or state, it came to be repetitive and to lose it essential reason for being: shock. Whatever his pictures lack in bizarre quality, Dali makes up for in his personal appearance, behavior and published statements. He enjoys a lively press and, seemingly, financial success. He is a showman who once joined in producing a surrealist girly show at the 1939 World's Fair.

But, while these explorations of the subconscious with the resulting impact on art were taking place, another sort of reaction to cubism had taken place in Paris. One group, not a school, but with a somewhat common intention, sought to go back to nature, to the color theory of the impressionists and the plastic theory of form found in Cézanne. They took the name of "Section d'Or" from a magazine named *La Section d'Or,* which unfortunately enjoyed only one issue. Artists such as Léger, Delaunay, de La Fresnaye, were at the van of the movement. With the advent of this group, a greater freedom and crossing over lines ensued. An escape from the rigid set of rules imposed by cubism was possible.

In Germany before the war, another sort of art was in development. Under the leadership of Franz Marc and Wassily Kandinsky, a group emerged called the Blue Rider School. This group published a yearbook replete with revolutionary and original articles with wide-ranging interests in many aspects of art. The intention of the publication was perhaps best summed up by Franz Marc in his exhortation, "Traditions are all very well, but what matters most is creating, not living one." Out of this group came the expressionists, whose art had such an untimely end with the advent of the war. The work of a few members of this group is covered elsewhere in this book.

After the war, an important segment of the German creative life centered in the Bauhaus School. The school was founded in 1919 by a leading architect in Germany, Walter Gropius. Originally in Weimar, it moved to Dessau, where it remained until closed by the Nazis. The Bauhaus concept was a romantic ideal disguised as a realistic approach to the new art of construction. As a matter of fact, this romanticism resulted in a marked separation of approaches on the part of the Bauhaus architect-designers and the Bauhaus painters—so much so that the group known as *De Stijl*, a group with almost the same aims founded two years earlier in Holland, thought the Bauhaus to be contradictory in theory and practice.

The Dutch school, founded by the painter Theo Van Doesberg together with Piet Mondrian and the architects J. J. Oud, Rietveld and Van Eesteren, had as a central esthetic a belief in an abstract representation of all form as constructed in an unorganic, geometrical arrangement. Against this rigidity of belief was the work in the Bauhaus, where more individuality of personal approach was possible. While the architects held this geometric esthetic as the dominant characteristic, the painters were expressionists running the whole gamut of style from fantasy to geometric expressionism. So at the time the architects Gropius and Breuer were creating their geometric buildings and chrome furniture, the painters Klee, Kandinsky and Feininger were involved with the production of a broad spectrum of theories and kinds of painting.

While the artists all over Europe were in a brouhaha of exploration, exhortation and condemnation of one another, something was happening to ordinary man as well.

The war had taken its toll, not only of artists but of all society, and rebellion against previously accepted standards for morals and manners was in the air. In the United States it was the era of the flapper—of looser moral attitudes through petting, of leaving off corsets, of short dresses and of stockings rolled down below the knee. Women's suffrage in the United States was imminent and woman was demonstrating that she was going to be heard from. She was eradicating the overt feminine symbols by tying a bandeau over her breasts in order to give her chest a flat and boyish look. She bobbed her hair. She took to smoking and drinking in public places. And at the same time, as a feminine gesture of revolt, women began the heavy use of cosmetics heretofore associated with prostitutes and the bolder demimondaines.

All of these changes were symptomatic of the desire to be free, to destroy old restrictions and to be ever young and gay. Youth was the ideal, and everyone could at least associate with young ideas in manners and morals. A great social experiment was launched with calamitous moral repercussions. Prohibition had been made the law of the land. Flouting the law became socially acceptable, even desirable, since it was a symbol of independence and rebellion from fuddy-duddy concepts of morals, law and order.

The breakdown of earlier standards was rushing along at a furious pace. Sex was brought out into the open in newspapers, magazines, books and the theater. It was the heyday of juicy scandals, riotously reported by the newspapers. Daddy and Peaches Browning were photographed in their bedroom. The play *The Captive* publicly brought attention to the fact that homosexuality existed. The same news was brought to the masses through Radclyffe Hall's book, *The Well of Loneliness. Lady Chatterley's Lover* was published and banned.

The attitude prevalent toward manners and morals was extended to art. Since it was important to be young, the new and cheerful young ideas in art were welcomed as an extension of the youth ideal. In addition, the new art represented a considered attack on middle-class morality—a welcome ally against a common adversary. Home decoration reflected this bent. Our dancing daughters were seduced in penthouses furnished with chrome tubular furniture and sky-scraper chests of drawers in rooms painted in violently prime colors. On the walls were African sculpture or modern paintings or the reproductions of them.

For the first time, the artists' rebellion was joined by a division of the one-time enemy, the middle class. An ever-increasing band of believers was forming up. In the United States there was still no conviction that anything first-class could come out of the United States (in art). It was to Mecca—Paris—that they still turned. Transatlantic visitors brought back the word of trends, brought back pictures and smuggled in banned books. The artists had planted a fifth column right in the middle of the middle class.

This group was ready to accept most of the art offered, including the new music. Debussy, Ravel, Stravinsky were the epitome of musical adventurers and therefore to be supported. But in music an enormous change was imminent. Music had slowly evolved through centuries on a major-minor tonal system. There had been several breakthroughs in evolutionary developments before. In the beginning of the 17th century, music had broken with the system of church modes and adapted a contrapuntal, linear system. About the middle of the 18th century there was another great change to the sonata form. On that form, astounding edifices of chordal structures and wide-ranging chromaticism had been built. It was as though the ultimate had been reached—there was seemingly nowhere to go.

Arnold Schönberg created a new atonal order by his use of the 12-tone scale and through his work the serial system was developed. There were other contemporary composers who also were exploring ways out of the impasse. Paul Hindemith, Béla Bartók and the indefatigable Igor Stravinsky were all brilliantly going their individual ways, but it was left to Schönberg and his lieutenants, Alban Berg and Anton Webern, to create a wholly new system—a system so new and revolutionary that the present-day composer has not yet exhausted, or for that matter seemingly understood, its potentials.

On the other hand, the audience has not been able to adapt itself to hearing it. It is a system so complex and obscure that today, according to Iain Hamilton, the contemporary English composer-critic, many young composers have avidly seized upon it to hide their poverty of true inventiveness.

In Austria new music was being born, in Germany a new architecture was being created, and in Paris that old magician and genius Picasso was making his own personal odyssey through his own styles, totally indifferent to his audience and yet by some form of sorcery never losing contact with them. Once he was secure within himself, he was able to maintain his communicative powers despite his abrupt changes in style. His originality never intruded into his relationship with his audience. He developed a decorative cubism, neoclassicism, giantism and his own form of expressionism. In Paris at the same time, the sculptors had discovered cubism and started their own journey through different postures of arrival and departure in both esthetics and originality.

This was the situation in Europe until a new displacement of the artist took place. It came with the advent of Hitler and the Nazi movement. Artists and

architects, composers and poets from Central Europe
fled to Switzerland, England, France and the United
States and began the formation of an international
style. This period of partial disruption and political
consciousness ended with the complete disruption and
destruction of World War II.

If disillusionment, despair and disgust had been the
heritage of former wars, the aftermath of World War II
was to leave all men with the conviction that life was
utterly meaningless. The shocking demonstration of
destructive power by a single primitive bomb in Hiro-
shima was appalling. What awful things lay ahead?
The feeling was shared by all men—artists and men
of the lower, middle and upper classes. The artist had
no way out from his despair. He had little room to
maneuver. He had no place to go. He was shorn and
bereft.

Heretofore in such a situation his immediate reaction had been to lash out against the institutions
which made such things come to pass. The focus of his
attack had always been the middle class, which by its
insensitivity, greed and materialism brought such
things about. But now there were newer, unnamable,
implacable forces around. It was a mysterious "they"
or "it" against which there was no defense. It went by
the name of progress or of ideology. It could not be
attacked, its face and corpus were unclear. Now the
old enemy no longer existed. Everyone was on the
same brink of annihilation or, at best, subject to the
same sort of depersonalization.

The artist cannot fall back on a fight against the
lack of understanding for today he is smothered with

understanding. He can paint with chicken shit like Dubuffet or throw paint on canvas like Jackson Pollock, or, like Pierre Boulez or Karlheinz Stockhausen, record a series of sounds lying somewhere between mathematically arranged natural noises and electronic signals. As soon as one of these works, guaranteed to bewilder and amaze, is produced, then from the factories of understanding, articulate spokesmen, equipped with magical forensics, explain, re-explain and soothe and one is made to feel guilty if the immediate meaning cannot be grasped. Dada has gone from being an art of the absurd and remonstrance to becoming a sacred icon.

On the stage the meaninglessness is acted out for us in the plays of Beckett and Ionesco and we beat our breasts in half-understanding grief. The artist, his traditional enemy gone, has turned his despair inwardly, into anti-humanism and anti-art.

Cavafy, the Alexandrian Greek poet, in a haunting poem tells of a great cultured city about to be taken over by the barbarians who have laid siege to it for many years. Amid the strange feelings of relief that come with the final act of surrender comes the whispered news. The barbarians are not coming. The focus of existence had been the struggle against the barbarians. Now there were no more barbarians. What now?

The artist no longer has his barbarians. He must now manufacture them. He has so many freedoms and so much understanding that he suffers from the tyranny of absolute choice.

Art has become the art of this moment—a thing of fashion, a completion unto itself, with only a present, no past and perhaps no future. Painting art has become an act of self-discovery, uninvolved with anyone but the artist himself—a graphic record of a period on his couch or the result of the manipulation of a giant Ouija board. It is noncommunicative and unrecognizable, a private calligraphy with meaning to none. Even the explanations are couched in relatively remote metaphysics.

Thomas Hess, the art critic, describes action painting as having "transformed [painting] into the mechanics of man-the-machine. . . . Action painting has to do with self-creation or self-definition or self-transcendence; but this disassociates from self-expression which assumes the acceptance of the ego as it is, with its wound and its magic. Action painting is not 'personal,' though its subject matter is the artist's individual possibilities."

Harold Rosenberg explains that "the new action painting [is] of the same substance as the artist's existence. The new painting has broken down every distinction between art and life." The attempts to bring a rational explanation to meaninglessness by articulate messiahs is delivered with so much evident intensity and sincerity as to frighten the timid questioners into silence. Rosenberg, in an explanation of the new creativity in action painting, describes it thus: "The painter no longer approached his easel with an image in his mind; he went up to it with material in his hand to do something to that other piece of material in front of him. The image would be a result of this encounter."

If this were truly an encounter, then the fights were

fixed, because all the pictures turned out with the decision going to the artist. The artist never lost, the fix was in. Even while Hess, Rosenberg and other masterly articulators were making it all plain, action painting was being choked to death by self-explanation and a new group of neo-Dadaists were taking over, the pop painters, even more overtly anti-esthetic. The critics are in the clear, however. Newness is what counts, not what the newness happens to bring.

What is happening to painting is happening in sculpture and in architecture as well. In architecture this antihumanism is bewildering since the essential concept of a building must be concerned with shelter. The considerations of the building as a sculptural form now push its consideration as shelter into the background, often calling for materials which the chemist has not yet invented, and so the architect turns to the nearest available. When he needs a new plastic, he settles for inadequate concrete. Sometimes the building meets the needs of its human function, more often it does not. As a matter of interest, a leading architectural avant-gardist, in an address to an A.I.A. meeting in Miami, held out the theory that the surpassing architectural monuments of man are antifunctional and therein lies their secret. The last inversion of the phrase has become "function follows form."

Music has become a prickly private art. Dodecaphony and its offspring, serial music, are unreachable and impenetrable. They still follow Handel's injunction to the composer to "hit them in the ear," but in most cases this has assumed the proportions of an assault. It is an attack from some remote world far removed from Mozart's credo, "Music . . . must never offend the ear; it must please the hearer, in other words, it must never cease to be music."

While our musical future is being spun out in some electronic studio, there is a raging vogue of music as distant from this cold ideal as it is possible to be. It is operating at three levels of acceptance. For the young and uninvolved, there is the music with the beat—jazz—(a) rock and roll and (b) the jazz of Thelonius Monk, Miles Davis, John Coltrane, King Pleasure and others. For the involved, young, old or beatnik, it is jazz of variety (b) and folk songs.

For the intellectual, the current magic names are Vivaldi and Frescobaldi, Josquin des Prez and Heinrich Schütz. Baroque music is the vogue and the popularizers are reaching farther back into the Renaissance and dipping into the few musical documents of the late Gothic which are extant. It is a pity indeed that musical notation came into being so late, or we could all be orgiastic together at a replay of the Eleusinian mysteries to the accompaniment of the original instruments.

As a matter of fact, the public will listen to anything except the music of the serious avant-garde composer. The public listens to one of these works as an act of obedience and then rushes off to the past or for something to which it can stamp its feet. It can be argued that this has been the fate of the recent composer from Debussy on, but the willingness to understand was not as great as it is now. The public wants to understand, but it is not given an opportunity by the artists, who wish to exclude it. The tragic fact is that a vast and growing separation exists.

A curious nonrelationship exists between the audiences for modern music and modern painting. One could assume that the audience for modern painting, in its apparent eagerness to identify itself with the new, would be equally drawn to the music of today. But this is not the case. The audiences for the music is minuscule in relationship to that for the painting. One aspect of the situation is strange in that music always has been abstract and therefore does not have to break down the instinctive rejection of nonrepresentationalism which we find in painting.

Beyond the fact that today's music is more austere and complex and that the human ear may not be able to adapt itself as readily as the eye, the major difference lies in the nature of the two arts. The public at large is much more aware of the existence of modern painting. Communication through print and broadcast, and imitation of aspects of painting in decorative accessories, brings news of painting into everyday living. In addition, a painting can be contained in a look, and if nothing else, it is colorful and decorative. Modern music not only is difficult to listen to, but there is no way to possess it. It exists in time. There can be no ownership of a one-of-a-kind with the reflected status that comes from that ownership. Nor can music be displayed as an artifact of one's living.

Meanwhile, for painting, a whole edifice of professional supporters has risen—the mandarin society and its institutions, museums, universities, fashion magazines, art dealers, artists, fashion designers, architects, designers, decorators and critics. The common article of faith is that art is new and that understanding is limited to the inner circle. When too many people share the secret, it is time to move on to something new.

By a strange twist of fate, the vanguard in opposition to the dullard middle class no longer is the artist. He has become an instrument. The mandarin group, for reasons and needs of its own—status, power and the hunger for self-identity—uses him to denigrate the great intellectually unwashed. Modern painting is becoming increasingly seen if not universally respected. Anyone who wants to count must get in on the act. It is fashionable, and ours is a wealthy and fashionable society. Modern art has become a culture badge. Because of the fashionable response it is used to increase the take by museums, banks, insurance companies, soft-drink manufacturers and suppliers of basic packaging supplies.

The forces of separation have been operative only for a little more than a century, but they already have taken art a long way away from man. The single most important imperative is that art must be original. If it has that quality, then nearly anything else can be forgiven. And yet, in the magnificent history of art, several men emerge who are the antithesis of such a belief. Johann Sebastian Bach, who today shines out like a beacon of genius, was not a very original man. He was still working in the contrapuntal linear style when those of his time were excitedly exploring the sonata form. He borrowed themes wherever he could find them. Now, in the compressed perspective of time, it makes little difference to anyone but music historians how late or early he was in terms of originality. What counts is his work. How important is originality in the summation of Mozart's work? He borrowed his opera form from the Italians, but what came out was his own.

Some erudite scholars have recently made us aware of a French composer of 150 years ago, Charles Valentine Alkan. He is the private enthusiasm of a few musicologists. They point out that in his work can be heard innumerable passages which anticipate those found later in Chopin, Berlioz, Liszt and, much later, Mahler. This makes him an originator, yet he is unknown. Hearing his work, one becomes aware of the reason for his lack of fame despite his indicated originality. If an artist is a Beethoven, Wagner, Michelangelo or Leonardo, great originality is a facet of his development and adds stature to his work for succeeding generations to enjoy, but what makes his work great is the content which that originality helped create.

Originality as an end in itself is self-defeating. Granted that originality is a precious element in art— without it the central wonder and excitement is lost. But when the desire to be original overwhelms every other quality that must in one way or another be present in a lasting work of art, then we are beset not so much by original sin as by the sin of originality. Time has its own methods of discounting originality. When the time period is compressed, it becomes an interesting sport for the record keepers to know who started first. It is the arrivers we remember.

Occasionally living ghosts come back from the past to remind us that *plus ça change, plus c'est la même chose.* In a recent interview, an aging Man Ray sneered at the namby-pamby, puerile attempts by our present-day innovators to astound, and incidentally demonstrated the importance that he and his time placed on shock value. When asked how he compared this time and his own glorious bygone days, he said: "We really put their eye out then."

Part 2

Part. 2

The Decline of Discipline

Not long ago several impious broadcasters at the BBC perpetrated an irreverent hoax on the musical community of Britain. An agglomeration of random nonmusical tape sounds were pieced together with great care to avoid any musical idea in its continuity. The result of this otic salad was named "Mobiles," a name loaded with exciting promise of new forms in a truly modern idiom. A composer was invented and announced as being a Pole who, for political reasons, refused to reveal himself publicly.

Another dimension of interest was thus added, for beyond the protection afforded the pranksters by the

obscurity of the artistic life in the Iron Curtain countries was this tantalizing show of the unconquerable
and restless contemporary spirit welling up in the
Philistine art world behind the dark frontier.

Having paved the way for a wide hearing, the in-
ventors of the mélange had it played over the BBC.
It was seriously reviewed by music critics and musicians, but not a single person identified it as a piece
of non-art. Several musicians found it stimulating and
full of ideas, as did most of the critics. Absurdly few
thought it an inferior work. However, each opinion
was expressed in the context of a performance of a
serious work of art.

The essence of this prank is an indication of the
present state of art, a state in which the disciplines of
art have been progressively thrust aside until all the
signposts of recognition are gone. The borders between
art and non-art have become blurred and indiscern-
ible, and it is no longer possible to distinguish between
them, an error impossible to conceive in the age of
Mozart.

Let us be explicit. In this case the concern is not a
quarrel with the qualitative judgment of misguided
critics. This is not a repeat of the Paris riot at the first
playing of *Le Sacre du printemps,* nor the Ruskin-
Whistler paint pot flung in the public face, nor should
it be confused with the journalistic uproars in the early
days of the impressionists. In each of these cases the
quarrel lay in the fact that the artist's work did not
meet the standards set by the art establishment of the
time, and the charges ranged from bad painting to
charlatanism. But even at that time, despite the ill-

considered attack of some, the artist had a few technically based supporters, for at least bench marks existed on which judgments could be based. In the case of the BBC hoax, all the standards from which discernment could start had disappeared, and trained listeners, having become wholly dependent upon purely sensate reactions, were unable to expose or even suspect a nonmusical prank.

It is not the intention to use this incident as proof that strange and different works are insincere, or that nonrecognition makes a work non-art. The BBC hoax illustrates rather that with the exception of an artist's signature and indications of his stylistic method, we have few signposts of recognition. With value judgments based solely on sensate reaction, we become part of a ritual cult relying upon the revelatory laying-on of hands of the high priests who elevate a work to the status of art or doom it to ignominy as a daub.

Art, which began as a recording by primitive man of the world around him, evolved into an art as it became an ideational projection of beauty, emotion and perception within a framework of discipline. In the long history of art these disciplines have changed, academies have risen and fallen as the artists of a period rebelled against the constrictions of a given set of rules. None the less, great and beautiful art has flourished within the disciplines. Some disciplines are mandatory, some imposed by the artist himself. Certainly those which relate to physical man are mandatory. A plastic or graphic work must be arranged so that it can be visually comprehended by the human eye. Music is arranged by pitch and rhythm to be held by the human ear. And architecture, other than monumental or ritual, must afford human shelter.

As these arts evolved, a more sophisticated set of rules came into being so that the work filled more than the basic physiological requirements. Optic laws of bodies in space came to be understood and were recognized by expanded graphic disciplines. In music, the original harmonic and rhythmic rules were altered so that the original simple combinations of sounds and rhythms could be enlarged and invested with more power and still be made comprehensible to the ear. And the development of new structural principles gave architecture impressive power and beauty.

As art progressed from reportage to the paramount expression of the human spirit, other disciplines were developed to give deeper expressivity within the needs of its society. Iconographical systems were developed and replaced as the aims and beliefs of a society changed. Erwin Panofsky in *Meaning in the Visual Arts* devotes a section to the history of proportion in the human figure as a reflection of historic style. Using such an example, history also illustrates the interrelation of disciplines in the graphic and plastic arts as they evolved through various ages. In addition it demonstrates how these disciplines, while essentially limiting the artist, still provided him with a framework within which to build a great and continuous art. Panofsky's work traces the changing disciplines over a vast span of centuries.

Painting and sculpture in Egypt were used for ritual purposes and were part of an architectural system. Even when used for decoration, the influences remained the same. In the depiction of the human figure the artist was not concerned with a fleeting variable such as movement, but rather the figure was conceived as a constant and fixed ideograph. The esthetic ideal reduced the movement of kneeling or walking into a fixed symbol. It was a movement eternally arrested. A man kneeling to the king forever kneels to him.

Since the figure was not conceived as an individual but rather as an archetype, a stylistic proportion was developed to serve as a framework for the artist. Papyri exist which show that an 18-square grid was used on which to draw the figure. Later, for greater refinement, the grid was increased to 22 squares. The ankle, hip, shoulder and chin all intersected a recurring point of the grid each time a figure was drawn. The same proportion was used to illustrate simple movement. Each kind of element—a sphinx, an animal and a human—had its own separate grid constructed of a different number of squares.

The Egyptian discipline of proportion held until the emergence of the classical Greek art. In this glorious art is reflected the appreciation of man as a human being rather than a ritual figure, and its disciplines shifted to meet that esthetic ideal. In the telescoping of time, the shifts look abrupt. However, Diodorus of Sicily tells how two sculptors of the sixth century B.C., Telekes and Theodoros, each made a separate part of the same ritual statue, one in Samos and the other in Ephesus. When brought together, the two parts fitted perfectly. This was possible under the Egyptian method of designing to an established grid. It would be impossible in succeeding centuries. In these latter centuries the work was not as rigidly controlled by method, so that two men working separately would have little likelihood of matching their results. But the fact that it was possible in the sixth century B.C. indicates the penetration of the Egyptian method and discipline into another society and time.

Greek art, in order to achieve its respect for man, had to free itself from the mechanical insistences of Egyptian rules. The art became more concerned with a vital present rather than an eternal constant. The Greeks were interested in capturing movement. So Greek art escaped from a rigid 18-to-22-grid system and developed a system of its own which permitted greater freedom of movement for the individual figure. It was a system of fractional proportion between parts of the body, and while the system allowed any natural movement, there was an exact relationship between parts of the body set down in a scale such as:

1. Hollow of throat to crown of head   ¼ body length
2. Crown to chin   ⅛ body length
3. Breadth of chest   ¼ body length
4. Hand (wrist to tip of middle finger) ¹⁄₁₀ body length
5. Length of foot   ⅙ body length

In addition, a scale with mystical significance was drawn in which the figure when erect and with arms outstretched filled a square. The figure when spread-eagled filled a circle with the navel as center.

In addition to the development of a proportional system which permitted the artist to show movement with greater freedom, the Greeks recognized the existence of certain optical laws. They employed a rudimentary method to approximate the illusions of foreshortening. The story is told of an Athena by Phidias which the artist carved with the proportions of the lower part of the statue much smaller than those of the upper part. However, when the statue was set up, the relationship between the upper and lower part was harmonious. Phidias had recognized foreshortening due to aerial perspective and had adapted his proportions to overcome a potentially disturbing optical illusion.

This same recognition of optical laws was carried on into architecture. The Greeks curved the lines of architraves and high pedestals to make them appear straight to the eye. In arcing the line they corrected an optical tendency for a straight line to dip because of aerial perspective. Corner columns of a portico were given another thickness in order to make them seem to have the exact dimensions of the inner ones, overcoming another observed optical illusion.

The Greek theorists systematized proportion and optical rules within an essentially humanistic tradition. Their system was designed to appeal to the eye. What the figure appeared to be was the guide, rather than the recognition of some immutable concept to which appearance and reality must adapt themselves as in Egyptian art. According to the theorist Polyclitus, within this harmony of part-to-part lay the principles of beauty.

Byzantium was at the crossroads of Eastern and Western cultures. The social structure of this society was influenced by the power complexes of the East. No longer part of a democratic society, man as the center of his universe was denigrated and institutions took his place. Along with the absorption of these Eastern ideas came that of many aspects of Eastern culture. The flat plane as an esthetic ideal returned to Western art, copied from Eastern paintings.

Byzantine art basically was built around a system of planes which encompassed a modular method that reflected the tools of the artists—the compass and ruler. It was a return to a mechanical system more rigid than the Greek and less humanistic. It reflected the spiritual quality of its time even to its unit of proportional measurement. The face in Byzantine art is the essence of the spirituality. The body is sinful, clothed and hidden behind a stylistic façade, and it is the face that becomes the unit of measurement. So in the painters' manual of Mt. Athos is found the following scale of proportions:

Body	9 face units
Face	3 nose units
Torso	3 face units
Upper part of leg	2 face units
Lower part of leg	2 face units

The face itself was built on three concentric circles with the center at the root of the nose. The inner circle outlined the eyebrows, cheeks and bottom of the nose; the middle circle defined the top of the head to the bottom of the chin. The outer circle extended from the pit of the throat to the periphery of the halo.

The Byzantine system of nine face units held well into the 18th century.

The Gothic system was structural, reflecting its magnificent architecture. The figure and its component parts were based on intersecting squares, triangles and circles. At first the figure conformed to the geometric construction but later, because of the desires for individual expression by the illuminators, painters and sculptors of the time, a range of naturalistic rendition was introduced, still controlled by the geometric shape but allowing for freedom within the form.

The Renaissance fused all the former systems into a glorious one of its own. In the rebirth of humanism it sought to combine mechanical rules of proportion and metaphysical rules of universality into a new esthetic ideal. Human proportion still was built around nine face units. The figure was minutely measured and ideal proportions for each part of the body were set down. In its magical construction it still retained the figure within the circle and square, but moved the center of the circle-universe from the navel to the crotch—they either had longer legs or were a sensual people indeed.

In the brilliant exposition by Panofsky we can find more fully explored the changing disciplines of succeeding ages as they relate to one aspect of graphic art—proportion. But disciplines exist in all aspects of art. The Renaissance was a period bursting with exploration and artistic invention. Whole new esthetic principles were explored and systematized into disciplines. Musicians set secular poetry to music in early operatic forms, freeing words and music from the convention of liturgical use, using them in forms compatible with its new purpose. Poets sang of human love, manners, metaphysics, setting new literary forms.

But it was in painting and sculpture that the greatest

explosion of wholesale genius took place. Within this seeming anarchy of personal expression were powerfully controlling disciplines. The artists of the period developed rules relating to the picture plane to insure compositional strength of conception. Rules of triangulation, linear, on the surface plane and dimensionally receding in depth into the picture, were established. Optic laws controlling value and chroma of colors were explored and set down. In the north of Italy in Venice, and still farther north in the lowlands, the effects of light and atmosphere were studied and conventions for the usage of color came into being. There is a direct line of inheritance between the Venetian painters and the great French impressionists. In Germany and Flanders two great technicians, Dürer and Van Eyck, developed new disciplines of craft based on discoveries of technique and form. Restlessly, each succeeding generation sought to develop principles and methods of its own to achieve greater expression in conformity with its own needs.

By the middle of the 19th century the revolt against the academies was in full career, concurrent with the revolutionary uprising against vested political systems. Artistic conventions were slowly thrown off, one by one. Still, a self-imposed discipline was recognized by the artist. No longer concerned with his subject to the degree held by former generations, he sought through a new grammar of form to express three-dimensional experiences while preserving the two-dimensional plane. The continuing search in this direction gradually evolved into cubism and then abstraction. Another search was in color, ranging from impressionists through pointillists, Fauvists, German expressionists, and eventuating in a theorist painter such as Kandinsky, in whose paintings the separate lines of exploration of color and form met to result in a forerunner of abstract expressionism.

Despite the fact that earlier rules were thrown away by the handful by each succeeding generation of painters intoxicated by their discoveries, it is significant to note the recurring persistence of the Renaissance rules. In the work of two of the most significant and influential painters of the immediate past and present, Cézanne and Picasso, we can see a direct line of descent from the French classicist Poussin.

Disciplines and systems are not restricted to Western art. They are the underlying strength of other cultures. To Western ears, Hindu and other Eastern music may sound like a convocation of cats or like a recording made in a sawmill. But underneath their strange tonal systems, strange to our ears, is a rhythmic structure as precise as a mathematical equation. Beneath the poetic and sensitive surface of Chinese and Japanese painting is a firm structural system of composition. A very rigid discipline is observed during the traditional Japanese poetry contest called Haiku. A cardinal rule of this lovely contest is the form in which beauty is expressed. It must be a nature poem of just 17 syllables.

Disciplines in art are not legislated into being, nor are they an edict of a divine father. These disciplines come from the artist himself in response to his own needs for a framework of creativity. Georges Braque expressed his needs most succinctly in the statement:

"I like the rule, the discipline which controls and corrects emotion."

Another artist who had a similar respect and pride in the discipline of his craft was the poet Paul Valéry. He said that nothing would please him more than to be required to write a poem of a given number of lines, even of words and letters, for in this way he could demonstrate his craftsmanship. Undoubtedly, beyond the scatological titillation, the strict form accounts for the endless fascination with limericks.

In spite of the demonstrated need for a disciplined framework, the overwhelming importance placed on originality as the principal component of art today to the exclusion of beauty, communication or any of the other time-honored aspects of art has thrust the exercise of discipline aside. Art, therefore, has entered a twilight zone in which nothing seems important but the artist's urge for identification. This hurtling from style to style, with shock and attention-getting as its main purpose, has brought us to the era of ape paintings, crushed automobiles and anti-art, a time when recognition has become a form of revealed religion, when the work itself is threatened with immediate destruction by the undisciplined use of materials which chemically destroy one another in combination, so that the startling effect disappears shortly after it is achieved.

Man is a societal creature who has learned up until now to survive by creating disciplines and therefore generally has taken steps to eliminate or change threatening excesses. The decline in discipline today, however, has its roots in the immense changes to society which have been taking place in the last century. The reasons for the decline in art disciplines grow from the artist's desire to escape from the confines of a supramechanized world. This desire has led him to search for means of greatly intensified self-expression. In his desire to escape from a society of which he despairs, the artist is responding to an unheeding urge to divorce man and art, to make art a thing in itself, for its own sake, separated and independent from man. The shifting disciplines which briefly emerge are based in some technical method or other, sometimes as esoteric as the dripping on of paint, or shooting containers of color placed on the surface with a rifle to achieve explosive effects. Such disciplinary systems become the nucleus for one isolated sect or other, enjoying brief notoriety and fame, but away from the mainstream of living.

Perhaps there is no longer any need or room for discipline in the future of art. The artist has every right to demand the freedom to explore, develop for himself. He does not need to be recognized to be an artist. Some work reflects the opinion that art as we know it must be destroyed in order to be reborn. On the other hand, it is difficult to escape the feeling that such destruction is unwarranted when the purpose seems mainly to provide the enjoyment of novelty and a device by which the mandarins gain separation and status through their identification with the results of that destruction.

The loss of discipline attacks the very basis of art, not only in the loss of the signposts of recognition that differentiate between art and anti-art as in the case of the BBC hoax, but in that it creates discontinuity and injures logical development. The anarchy which results from the casting off of all disciplines is in direct contravention to man's innermost instinct for continuity and survival. Man, who in our collectivized society has surrendered his identity and power of individual decision and is now faced with another symbol of his loss of continuity in present-day art, can only look on, uncertain if it is a joke or a calamity. He does not know whether to howl with laughter or with tears.

Technology and Technique

It was Winston Churchill who once said, "We first shape our buildings, and then they shape us," and as usual in the case of a Churchill aphorism, it has meaning beyond its immediate context. Unquestionably the houses and cities built by man have in the end shaped his life. So have all of his institutions and societies. But of all the edifices that man has erected, his technology, that unsurpassed marvel, the result of his imagination and thought, has done more to alter and shape his life than anything which has happened to him since Adam ate an apple and Adam's people lost their belief.

Technology and science have become so sophisticated and exotic that man is on the verge of bursting through the borders of his own planet into the awesome worlds of space. Technology has brought him countless physical benefits and brought relief from the ordinary rigors of existence, but unfortunately has not helped to bring any clarity to the purpose of living. Quite the reverse is true, for the urgency once given to these purposes through the necessities of survival has been dulled by the opiates of material comfort. This material largesse has led philosophers to despair at the losses to meaning in human society. Not the least of these losses is the dehumanizing effect of technology on art, thereby compounding man's alienation and estrangement.

The direct effect of technology has been to compress the individual into mass man. The techniques of industrial production no longer require individual skills as the production engineer divides the work load into the separated component tasks in some version of the assembly line. The recognition of an individual's contribution and accomplishment is no longer apparent, so that the psychological rewards accruing from a direct expenditure of labor are no longer felt. The technology itself has become so involved and specialized that it requires a depth of knowledge and skill beyond the capacities of ordinary man. He must, therefore, accept the position of doing what he is told without comprehension. The very environment in which this sort of employment takes place reflects the ant-hill nature of a community which labors without the opportunity for self-expression or the maintenance of self-identity.

Curiously, in 1946 Elton Mayo[1] proved through a most interesting series of experiments conducted for the Western Electric Company that workers in an old plant who were made conscious of their own individual contribution and who had some control over the appearance of their surroundings consistently outproduced the workers in a new plant who had the advantages of a modern assembly line. The effects of his experiment have been far-reaching on industrial practice, but alas have had little effect on physical environment. The control of the shape and content of the physical plant and structure are in the hands of artist-architects who reflect the scientific imagery of technology rather than the desire to develop those factors of human necessities rediscovered in Elton Mayo's studies. The iconography of technology has permeated all of the arts. The net effect has been to make it an added factor in the alienation of man and art.

While art seems at times to be armed with a purpose and destiny of its own, not necessarily attuned to man, the artist is a man—a man who shares all of mankind's fears, needs and pressure. Like his fellow man, he is enthralled by the audacity and imagination implicit in the new technology, while at the same time he is uneasy at the effect it has on his society. The artist, with his sensitive gifts, is quick to sense and rebel against the loss to the individual as he is compressed into mass man. But

[1] *Human Problems of an Industrial Civilization* (New York: The Viking Press, 1960).

stronger than his fears are the attractions and fascination of technology, the physical manifestation of science. Above all, it is the absolute symbol of contemporaneity, and in identification with it lies the assurance that he, in his generation, contributes something important to the total flood of history. The existence and inexorable growth of science and technology seem to be outward proof of historical inevitability, an idea which has persisted in philosophy since Hegel.

There are assurances beyond contemporaneity in technology. In a world in which any truth is assailed with questions and doubts, only the truth in technology turns all doubts aside. Its truths, untroubled by ethical concepts or spiritual longings, are based on precise facts. So these truths exist, proved in the laboratory, supporting the new *deus ex machina* which is taking its place as the principal deity of its time, while belief in other gods falters. No wonder, then, that a vast number of artists are drawn to technology as a belief, inspiration and motivation, and it is equally inevitable that an opposing group will be moved to iconoclastic rebellion against this individual-destroying phenomenon.

These two opposing influences pervade much of art—one in imitation of and identification with technology, and the second in rejection of it. Though diametrically opposed, these two reactions to technology accomplish a common, if unfortunate, result. Both aid in further fashioning art into an instrument of alienation. These reactions have had a dehumanizing effect on sculpture, on architecture and on music, making them in turn unrecognizable, uninhabitable and unfathomable.

The artist's first reaction to technology is the surface imitation of its images or iconography, but soon the influences reach into the very essence of the form itself.

Sculpture

Such is the case in sculpture. The art of sculpture has always been inextricably involved with one technology or another. The very fact of constructing an armature, or the process of casting, demands a secure knowledge of the techniques which govern the nature of the art. But until the emergence of modern sculpture the technology was sublimated to the role of a technique in a particular medium. Its existence was not the dominant element of form or content.

With the work of Brancusi and of Archipenko the inherent technical nature of the material and its techniques began to assert itself and later to dominate the inner motivation of the art. Sculptured torsos lost their curvilinear subtlety and instead were constructed of polished, mechanical tubes and sheets. The geometry of the resulting forms reflected, in addition to the impact of cubism, the techniques of welding, brazing, and the mechanistic shapes of pipes, tubes and cubes. A parallel mechanistic image is seen in the work of the painter Fernand Léger.

These were the early manifestations of the influence of a technological society upon the imagery of sculpture and indeed on that of painting as well.

The figurative use of man as the principal element of content was adapted to reflect a technical society by altering the natural shape of the man to the shapes of technical products. But soon the penetration of technique and technology into the art of sculpture became deeper and more compelling. With the advent of constructivism, sculpture and modern technology became inseparable. The iconology of the art made a complete break with the past.

After holding a paramount position as the subject in content, man and his works were now no longer even present. The principal motivation behind content became the delineation of space. The linear representation of mathematical constructions formed the main body of motivating iconography. This precise imagery was accomplished by the use of materials utterly foreign to the millennia-old art of sculpture. Now modern technology overwhelmed the art as the hammer and chisel of Praxiteles and Michelangelo gave way to the welding torch and circular saw. The materials of the new technology—glass, metal sections of rod and tubes—became the materials of sculpture. Transparent plastic which could be formed and inscribed, wire and plate, all were present in startling combinations using all of modern technology's methods of welding-brazing, forging.

Since each succeeding creative generation seeks to find a place for itself, sculptors threw off the precise and limiting shackles of constructivism, although some still carry on, and sought for identity within expressionism. Just as in painting, where abstract schools have swung from the automatist improvisation of action painting to the controlled hard-edge school, so sculpture in its expressionistic development ranged from the effects achieved by partial or broken castings to the controlled arrangement of steel sheet and rods. The materials and methods are still those of modern technology, but the underlying idea of the content seems to be despair with the kind of society which brought the materials and methods into being.

A form of neo-Dada has arisen which features these materials in arrangements which heap contumely not only upon society, but upon sculpture as well. These are seen in the extremely avant-garde inventions of crushed automobiles, junk collages and mechanically moving or exploding contraptions.

These works are a far cry from the art which was a manifestation of the human spirit in its adoration, pride or comment upon beauty or sorrow. They show, none the less, a direct reflection of the technology and the anguish of our society. They have evocative power, although their many-leveled penetration of perception has been reduced. For the moment they give pleasure as novel arrangements of wire, plastic and metal, awakening the characteristics of response similar to those awakened by an article of fashion. And, as popular articles of fashion, they have the power to influence other phenomena within our society through a shared technology and an intriguing imagery.

Architecture

Technology has played a commanding role in the development of modern architecture. Modern architecture was made possible only through the technical developments of the last century and with this impetus was freed from the endless exploration of former styles as its principal esthetic motivation. The freedom gained is magnificent, and, in using the potential of invention and the properties of the new materials, architecture has made a gigantic leap forward. In terms of its effect on man, it is easily the most dominant of all modern arts. The architect has become an artist again instead of a decorator of façades or an artistically impoverished researcher into style. But even with this powerful impetus, when exercised in an atmosphere in which a prevailing esthetic shows little consideration for man, the influence of that esthetic is bound to affect architecture adversely.

In addition, a convention of architectural practice is extant which has an even more disquieting effect, namely, the division of labor between the architect and his engineer. With a few noteworthy exceptions, the engineer is the genie-servant of the artist-architect. In its engineering, architecture shows greatness. Engineers seemingly can work out any problem imposed. This leaves the architect free to exercise any whim of form, secure in the knowledge that his good genie will work it out.

One influence governing these whims today is the impact of contemporary sculpture. Architecture was once called the mother of the arts. Painting and sculpture were the final adornment placed upon or within its precincts. For that matter, there was little painting free from architecture before the 15th century and little sculpture of the same uninvolved nature before Donatello. Now sculpture has assumed an influential position in establishing a new grammar of form.

The fact that sculpture and architecture use the same kinds of materials, and to a degree share the same methods and tools in working with these materials, provides a common starting point. The great liberation of form inherent in sculpture is a constant invitation to the architect, whose free spirit is normally restricted by the necessity of human use and of structural requirement. Sculpture thereby becomes an influential source for motivation in the exploration of form by its invitation to free oneself from all restrictions and conventions. This is a fairly recent development in what was once orderly process. The changes to architecture came about through a response to the emerging technology.

The first approaches to modern architecture were unheralded. They were purely technical solutions and several buildings much ahead of their time were the result. The Crystal Palace by Sir Joseph Paxton in 1851 and the Galerie des Machines by Cottancin for the Paris Exhibition in 1889 are examples. Both exhibition buildings were designed with creative imagination and, in response to an emerging technology, they indicated new uses for iron and steel. But the lessons either were not learned or were not taken to heart, for the attitude soon shifted from engineering to esthetics.

Except for a brief interlude with the decorative characteristics of the *art nouveau,* the first esthetic recognition of the new technology at the turn of the century chose the direction of imitation of the spareness found in things mechanical. This took the form of abandonment of decorative detail contained within a simplified mass. Once this esthetic took hold, the influence of technology was intensified and parallel development of engineering and borrowed esthetics went forward.

The development of the steel skeleton building was a major architectural-engineering breakthrough. It first was used as an armature upon which masonry was hung. As the esthetic developed, the constructivist use of the material and exposure of the material's function gradually became an important part of the goal. The armature was therefore exposed and the outer skin of the building made as transparent as possible in order to expose best the skeleton and its structural means.

The effect of such a structure on human beings became a secondary consideration, although many persuasive rationales were developed. Inevitably, as this new esthetic form gained recognition, its influence spread into the furniture, artifacts and accessories which the building contained. The result was tubular steel furniture, clear glass tables, pipe-stemmed lamps and a large variety of complicated screen devices to keep out the glaring light which uncomfortably flooded the building.

Such a building and its furnishings have the power to make people conform. As Winston Churchill indicated, it helps form the very pattern of their living. Perhaps a Venusian sociologist sent here to observe and record the habits and mores of earthlings could, after peering into the windows of a contemporary dwelling, send back the following penetrating analysis of a mealtime ritual: "At meals the diners eat clear soup from crystal bowls placed upon a clear glass table, in order to look at their feet." This may be a *reductio ad absurdum,* but it is no more absurd than the esthetic which, when pushed to dehumanizing extremes, brings absurdity into our lives. We live with these absurdities without recognizing them as being ridiculous, especially when a ruling style overwhelms our reason and sense.

We can see with clarity the fashionable follies of past generations, but blind ourselves to those we live with. From our vantage point in history we howl with laughter at a society in which men wore high starched collars whose pinpoints, like some gleaming if stationary St. Catherine's wheel, stabbed constantly upward into their throats. Yet some of our pacesetters will live in a contemporary house which is built around an extremely open plan, that is, a plan in which one function of living is open and adjacent to another function, designed with a minimum of walls and of separation. This total arrangement is contained in a cube of glass. Such a house is an outrageous affront to privacy, and those who live in it spend endless hours in enjoyment of their audacious avant-gardism and in devising methods by which a small measure of privacy can be salvaged. That is the trouble with a ruling style. A development like the glass wall was magnificent when kept in bounds of human use. When it is outrageously pushed for purely stylistic desires and casts human need aside, it is ridiculous.

In its earliest employment, the glass wall integrated the interior with the landscaping surrounding it. New aspects of beauty and a new dimension of living were its immediate results. Until this time the nearest thing to it in domestic architecture was the sliding screen paper wall of Japanese architecture. The ability to open a room to the outdoors gave Japanese architecture the beautiful quality of integration of interior and exterior beauty. However, in Japan's climate such an all-weather devotion to beauty demanded a Spartan dedication. In the case of the modern glass walls, the rigors of climate are tempered by the supporting techniques of heating and ventilating.

As the glass wall became an important part of the total grammar of new form and an esthetic desire to expose the armature or skeleton of the building became prevalent, the glass garden wall became a transparent curtain wall. Now those who live high up in these glass cages find that instead of being spiritually fulfilled by living in close visual proximity to the earth and its flora, they are perched in a high, transparent aerie. Most men share a basic fear of heights. The human nightmare, falling out of the tree, was now a daymare. The clear glass wall now has become a test of nerves. In their use of these buildings people show an intriguing sense of invention by developing layouts, uses of furniture, to interpose a barrier, real or psychological, between themselves in their nest and the yawning chasm outside.

Another and ancillary problem of the glass curtain wall has been the control of light. Until now more light had been eagerly sought. Suddenly methods to keep it out became urgent. Heat by direct radiation has become a problem which must be overcome by an abnormal tonnage of refrigerated air in circulation. Other solutions have been sought. One is the *brise soleil,* or sun break. This is a series of deep external shades generally made of masonry which act as light traps. In some cases these have had an unfortunate capacity for becoming radiators in themselves through the retention of daytime heat and radiating the absorbed heat until the load is dissipated. The most prevalent device is the interior screen, which not only shuts out the light, but the view as well, and curiously has negated the total esthetic purpose of transparency by creating an interior wall sheathed in external glass, so that it is only at night that the true esthetic purpose can be revealed. The glass wall is only one of the joint results of esthetic whim coupled with an obedient technology.

Another sort of dehumanizing result of the esthetic whim which places such an urgency on the expression of a transparent cubical volume has been the assemblage of work areas in open spaces rather than as formerly constructed, with interior divisions. The herding of people is a direct result. Here we find a direct physical expression in environment of the compression of the individual into mass man. Privacy, the sense of identity and contribution are lost in the regimentation of faceless automatons in repetitious tasks. Our technical society increasingly is forced to conform to the pressure of mechanical methodology. Our architectural environment increases this dehumanizing process rather than searching for methods to alleviate it. The prevalent architectural esthetic is more concerned with the problem of self-expression for the artist-architect through the employment of the new technology for his own end than with any concern for its effect on the human users of his work.

Music

In a field far removed from architecture the same double impact of esthetics and technology is taking place. Technology and technique have helped alter the sound of music. Music has always been an abstract art. Fundamentally its development has been based on changing techniques. Its power to move comes when the gateways to the mysterious, spiritual and esthetic reservoirs deep in men are struck open by chords of response and the emotions flood. The sound of our music may have changed, but its effect on men has not since this fourth-century comment of St. John Chrysostom was recorded in a medieval manuscript: "Musicke doth withdraw our mindes from earthly cogitations, lifteth up our spirits into heaven, maketh them light and celestial."

Throughout its development, music has been marked by its organization into increasingly complex systems. Each new direction has usually been greeted by the hoots and howls of the critics and experts of its day as being the final idiocy. Despite this, the systems of Wagner, Debussy, Stravinsky and Schönberg all persisted and eventually became dominant influences for succeeding generations of artists.

Up until Schönberg these systems had one great common denominator—they were organized within a tonal order. That is, the composition was arranged within a single key structure or in carefully considered shifts or modulation from one key to others. These shifts were made for dramatic mood or technical effects or simply to relieve monotony. Sometimes the music was arranged within modal systems which, by their very limitation of range, gave a spare and haunting quality to the resulting composition and its harmonies.

This tonality was the immediate pathway into the human consciousness through that sophisticated instrument—the human ear. As music became more absolute it threw off its dependence upon tonality. A strain was thereby placed upon comprehension, because the music demanded an immediate recognition of a complex technical system without the immediate vehicle of tonality. Formerly the reliance upon sensuous fulfillment of sound was accompanied by an intellectual recognition of the system employed but not wholly dependent upon that recognition. It is a triumph that the human ear and human responses have been able to adapt themselves to such increasingly complex systems as have succeeded one another.

The dual impact of the esthetic doctrine of "art for art's sake" and of modern technology has had an enormous effect upon contemporary music. Other than by the imitation of its sounds, there is no image of modern technology that music can transfer. Imitations of sounds within the framework of the existing traditional forms always existed. These ranged from the direct imitation of natural sounds, as found in the Beethoven imitation of a summer storm in his *Pastorale Symphony* or the Richard Strauss imitation of sheep in his tone poem *Don Quixote* to impressionistic suggestions found in the works of Wagner and Debussy.

Contemporary composers used the device of imitating the technical sounds of the new day. One example is the imitation of the little mountain locomotive by Heitor Villa-Lobos, a faithful mimicking of the recognizable rhythms and sounds in starting, stopping, running. It has immediate transferable sounds in the hiss and roar of the steam and of its whistle and bell. Honegger's *Pacific 231* is a tone poem of the same sort of subject, but with a mixture of realistic imitation and impressionistic indication. In Prokofiev's ballet score *Le Pas d'acier* there are few identifiable sounds to imitate. It is an abstract comment, an expressionist work; its musical motivation, its thematic material and treatment, all are colored by the composer's reaction to the crushing threat of an overpowering technology. Honegger's and Prokofiev's compositions are examples of two manners by which composers reflect, through imitation or expressionist means, their reaction to the technological world which surrounds them. In form and content, however, they are composed within the older tradition of music.

There are, however, more directly attributable influences of technology and mechanism on technique.

A curious example is Stravinsky's *Serenata in A*. The controlling element in its structure is time, not musical tempo, but physical time caused by the limitations of a mechanical instrument. It was written to fill two sides of a 78-rpm disk. A mechanical device, the gramophone, is the central factor of its form. As a reflection of a direct mechanical requirement, it is technically no different, although of perhaps a more exalted character, than composing for a movie sequence or a one-minute television commercial jingle.

The doctrine "art for art's sake" has granted freedom from traditional form. It carries on into music and has shown up in various ways. One method has been the employment of traditional instruments in novel ways to the accompaniment of natural or mechanical sounds used out of context and amplified beyond recognition. The communicative intention of this kind of music is entirely dependent upon a sensate response to unusual and provocative sounds used in novel combinations.

Excerpts from two reviews of a series of New York avant-garde concerts by Ross Parmenter and Raymond Ericson, printed in *The New York Times* in August 1963, are perhaps most telling in their description of a self-conscious avant-gardism in its attempts to gain attention but more importantly to indicate the extent of the break with the long tradition of music. They demonstrate the degree of credence given to Dada musical experiments by an audience which, at an earlier time and in a different state of doctrinaire esthetic preparation, tore up the chairs at the first playing of Stravinsky's *Le Sacre du printemps*. The first excerpt is from Ross Parmenter's column of August 27:

Last night it was the Pocket Theater's turn, and the star performer of the evening was Joseph Jones's self-playing percussion assemblage. It looked rather like a coat tree hung with a violin, a metronome, something that whirled and some wooden Japanese wind chimes.

While various parts of the assemblage were set in motion by the unseen Mr. Jones, Alison Knowles sat on the stage behind an upside-down wash basin. It had a little mechanism on top, and her activity suggested that she was using matches to try to thread a sewing machine.

It turned out that she was trying, unsuccessfully, to light a little steam engine, whose sound was meant to be part of the piece. But if the steam engine didn't work, everything else, including the clock, the two metronomes and the violin were activated at one time or another. And the wind chimes were kicked into motion when a little propeller beneath them began whirling.

With the ticks, the clicks, the whirling and the vibrations, the assemblage was pleasant to hear. And there was always the suspense that it might go up in flames like the Mexican firework towers called *castillos*. But that was not in the script, and Miss Knowles's matches were never intended to ignite the assemblage.[2]

This next excerpt is from Raymond Ericson's column of August 28:

Most of the program was given over to works where the means had become more important than the end. The means were often elaborate attempts by from one to three pianists to get unusual sounds out of their instruments. Frederic Rzewski, David Tudor and Mr. Zumbro were the three artists involved, and, as instructed by the composers, they managed many feats of ingenuity. Yet the static succession of tones and noises seemed singularly empty, valid only as experiments.

There were pieces in the manner of John Cage, notably Toshi Ishiyanagi's lengthy *Music for Piano No. 2,* for three pianos. The pianists, just as often plucking and thumping away at the instruments' innards as they were at the keyboard, resembled nothing so much as surgeons operating on the bowels of the pianos, to which the latter responded with occasionally excruciating squeals and groans of agony. Some of the effects were entertaining for their novelty and occasional beauty. Beyond that lay boredom.

"Action Music for Piano," by Alvin Lucier, a young American composer now teaching at Brandeis University, provided an interesting variation on "action painting." The pianist was directed to move his hands, fingers, knuckles, elbows, full arms—even chin—in various ways with relation to the keyboard, letting the notes respond where the action landed.[3]

These two reviews describe one kind of contemporary avant-gardism. The unconscious blackmail used against the noncomprehending musical audience is operative in the case of this music, just as it is in painting and sculpture. That audience shrinks at the name Philistine and dares not consider the music anything but "serious." Overlooked, naturally, are the former avant-garde experiments which have disappeared like the winter snow, leaving behind only an indulgent recollection.

Of far greater importance in the realm of technical change is the invention of the tape recorder and finally of electronically induced sound. These two inventions have changed the sound of music, its context and methods of composition. The prodigal

[3] © 1963 by The New York Times Company. Reprinted by permission.

mechanical abilities of the tape recorder, coupled
with the often nonmusical sounds used in contemporary composition, have radically altered the sound
of music. In addition, when these devices are used in
combination with the theoretical developments of
atonalism and serialism, a quality of sound completely
unrecognizable as music is the result. So much so
that when encountered by an unprepared listener
while turning the dials of a radio, he cannot identify
the nature and purpose of the sound. The human
nervous system responds to sounds whether they are
arranged in a recognizable musical sequence or not.
A potential therefore exists in bringing fresh power
to the musical art through the use of these sounds
and devices. However, with the present-day concentration on means, much of contemporary music is
more the work of laboratory technicians than the
richly human art of the older forms.

Any discussion of technology and its effect on art
is involved with the question of technique. No art is
possible without it. The crudest production of sound
or any visual manifestation implies a technique to
bring it into being. In recent years, because of the
shift in emphasis from the content of art to its own
inward contemplation, there has been an increasing
reliance upon technique as the essential *raison d'être*.
When, in addition, the artist functions in a society
possessed by a devouring appetite for originality, the
nature of technique changes. At a time when a particular technique has become the immediate hallmark
in the identity of an artist, to the exclusion of content
or expression, the pace of change increases in leaps

from day to day, each artist pushing yesterday's excess just a little further, in the need to establish his own identity. There is little else by which to recognize him. When technique becomes the principal motivation in the search for self-identity, and further, when the artist feels he must find that identity within the framework of his time, it must follow, as the night the day, that the artist will not only turn to technology for his motivation, but to its materials and methods for his technique.

Thus the sculptor's hammer and chisel have given way to the welding torch and the spools of wire and plastic. A Stradivarius gives way to a chassis loaded with dials, vacuum tubes and transistors. On the face of it there should be nothing wrong with such substitutions. The artist always has searched for new ways to express himself. This search always has brought about displacement of instruments and methods. In the current displacement, however, there is not only the strangeness normal to change, but a carry-over of the dehumanizing qualities of these new materials and techniques. Added to all of the foregoing is the fact that today art has little disciplinary requirement, whatever the technique.

Technique was once a measure of the artist's skills. Today nearly any kind of skill is acceptable because of the overwhelming demand for novelty and surprise. There is a great reliance upon sensate response. Accident and improvisation are no longer looked upon askance, but are encouraged. If, therefore, the free fall of soldering flux or the result of an imperfect casting makes for a series of interesting

splashes or an unusual lump, the avant-garde pounces
upon it as the next-to-the-last coming and eagerly
proclaims it to the world with all the trappings of an
annunciation.

If the polyphonic use of the human voice singing
in canon the praises of God was a good device, then
certainly a mechanical repetition of electronic sound
on tape with phrase following phrase in a mathematically engineered canon is equally valid. The fact
that the canon is in reality a demonstration of the
mechanical sophistication of the device called the
tape recorder and that the canon is just a mechanical
trick of recording the same phrase in endless succession with small separations in time is overlooked.
The true nature of the trick is hidden by the use of
a technical stunt in the image of an ennobled form.

The impact of technology and technique, of its
materials, inventions in uses which concentrate on
means, has changed the face of art. Again, this is not
all bad. Certainly not when it re-energizes art and
provides the artist with new ways to reach his fellow
man. What is bad is the uses to which these devices
have been put, so that the most important result has
been to estrange art and man. The process of estrangement goes on, unheeded and irresponsibly, with gathering momentum. Whole schools are founded on a
technical device, whether it be the accidental breaking of glass or wood, the worship of the glass wall
or the imitation of an old patina by the imperfect
finish of concrete.

Perhaps it is just a question of time until the
artists have run the gamut of exploration in new

techniques, materials and devices. Or perhaps the society that supports this self-conscious indulgence will tire of endless novelty and require again some relationship between society and its art. At such a time the impact and processes of technology and technique will be powerful tools of communication of emotion.

Part 3

Architecture

If the prophets of historical determinism are correct, then architecture in this technical society will develop along predestined paths, eventuating in a coldly rational people-container. Its regional character and adaptations to local needs will be lost in some collectivized methodology.

Roderick Seidenberg, in his book *Posthistoric Man,* points out that architecture is well on its way to this pellucid if barren state, for it already has lost its national identity and is organized into an international style which may perhaps be described as the science of space organization. For the moment at least, such a projection is too neat. In applying to architecture proofs that the traditional freedom of the individual is narrowed by the patterns of a collectivized society, and thus that the individual will lose not only his sense of inward autonomy but his freedom of choice and value as well, he overlooks the freedom of choice exercised by that irrational artist, the contemporary architect.

The latest turnings of architecture are not toward rationalism; in the Gestalt of our time, our buildings are becoming profoundly irrational people-containers. The artist-architect, in step with his fellow artists the painters and sculptors, is turning slowly away from his recent constructivist rationale to a form of expressionism as his centripetal drive. The sterile, hollow, constructivist glass house is becoming an expressionist concrete cave.

Thus the shift away from human concern and toward an emphasis on means, observable in the visual arts, is operative in architecture as well. With these other arts, and reflecting their impact, it shares in a dehumanizing role.

Modern architectural form, according to Matthew Nowicki, rests on a triple base—humanism, functionalism and construction. These all may be present in a modern architectural composition, but other than in a brief obeisance to plan, humanism is the least apparent of the elements which form the basis upon which contemporary structures are designed. Increasingly, the esthetics of style growing out of material and structural systems shoulder human values aside. Despite the fact that architecture should be intimately concerned with the physical aspects of human life, it sacrifices many of the requirements in its response to the overriding esthetic of the day. While sympathy can be developed for the metaphysical urges inherent in the art for art's sake philosophy extant in the visual arts, the design of a building for human use can recognize nothing short of design for people's sake.

Because the contemporary architect is blessed or cursed with a prodigal technology, almost anything he draws can be built. In attaining his esthetic goals, he has no disciplines except self-imposed ones adjusted to fit the occasion. The disciplines of former periods, the limitations of structural possibilities, have almost disappeared, so that he has almost complete freedom to indulge any whim of novelty he has in mind. In such a time, when a ruling esthetic which certainly is not people-oriented is dominant, the interests of human society in its structures and cities are not best observed. This extraordinary technology is being employed to achieve a variety of esthetic goals so that the architecture, as a result, is a triumph of technical skills. Within this technology is the potential of enormous environmental benefits to men. However, to quote Mumford again, "Modern architecture observes neither man's meteorological, biological nor psychological needs, much less human activity or personal needs."

Louis Sullivan's credo of form following function reached its apotheosis in Le Corbusier's often quoted, "The house is a machine for living." This was a people-centered conviction and brought forward a fresh appraisal of architectural necessity. It brought new concepts of plan relationship, of orientation and of fenestration. But shortly afterwards the function which controlled the form changed. It was no longer the function of use, but rather was interpreted to mean the function of a structural system. Now the break with a people-oriented motivation was sharp. From an exploration of forms to adjust to new patterns of living, the prime necessity was placed upon the exposure and definition of the structural system. This is an underlying element in all of the twists of style now current. Form still follows structural function, but again the definition of function was altered to reflect the function of the materials of the buildings. It remained this way for several years, during which time there was an explosion of glass cube buildings.

A constructivist's dream world has become a reality. Mammoth monumental sculptures are being erected all over the landscape, for this is the esthetic motivation behind avant-garde architecture today—a building is inhabited hollow sculpture. These buildings are everywhere, their metal frames, stark and elegant, glass cubes shining in their crystalline serenity, troubled only by the people who inhabit them. Alas, these benighted humans who cannot evolve as rapidly as the architecture.

The glass buildings have been the dominant esthetic for scarcely more than a decade and already, in direct parallel with the painters and sculptors, the artist-architects have exhibited the same cyclical shifts. They have begun to show their boredom with the limited potential of self-expression in that form of sterile constructivist art. We now are entering a period of rampant expressionism in architecture. Let the human beware! The favored material is reinforced concrete. It has the advantage of being plastic and lends itself to the curved and arched construction forms which offer the opportunity to escape from the rigid trabeated forms heretofore imposed by steel and glass.

With the freedoms granted by a brilliant ferro-concrete technology, a whole new range of architectural shapes is entering the grammar of form. A heavy concentration is on roof systems. Shell forms and folded plate structures are exciting to see and are a triumph of engineering skill. Also, of late, a great deal of attention has been placed on the sculptured quality of the outer skin. The expressionist search takes two separate directions, although motivated by the same esthetic requirement. It seeks to reintroduce the feeling of weight in the structure through the sculptured form of its outer walls. With the retreat from the smooth glass cube comes not only the reintroduction of massive projections and recessions in order to create strong light and shade, but in absolute contrast to the sleek glass material, a forming and pouring of the concrete to bring out rugose tactile qualities of the outer skin. In some quarters the name given to this ferocity in concrete is neobrutalism.

A noteworthy example is the Marseille apartment complex by Le Corbusier, a least happy solution by a very great originator. Unfortunately, the human occupant has fared little better in this 180-degree turn from the glass building. His quarters have become grottoes, where they were once hothouses. Heavy, intruding structural members occur where they do the occupant the least good. Outer walls bear only a remote relationship to the plan or the function of the fenestration. In a new interpretation of what is meant by integrity in architecture, as in the case of the Fine Arts School at Yale, an excessive and unfunctional number of floor levels were created in order to force the relationship of the protruding verticals and horizontals. These walls are composed as an expressionist, sculptured mural. There is slight recognition in the outer wall of the human use or of plan necessity.

It would have been an imaginative supposition indeed for anyone to have conceived the idea that architecture would be exploring expressionism in the middle of this century. All logic pointed to a continuation of the purist-constructivist rationale. There were isolated and contrary examples, but these hardly indicated any deviation in the mainstream of development. Significant as an early exception, but hardly making a major seminal impact, was the work of the Catalan architect Antonio Gaudi at the turn of the century. He was a sport, a one-of-a-kind, romantic and expressionist, with much of the overtones of the *art nouveau* in his ornamentation. His work is now exhumed by esoteric critics who, equipped with 20–20 hindsight, find prophetic portents in it.

Another isolated example is found in the early work of Erich Mendelsohn, whose Einstein Tower, built in flowing concrete forms, anticipates much of today's searching. However, Mendelsohn left his early style to join the ranks of the purist-constructivists, to whose style he contributed important work.

The true harbingers of the 20th century were the

engineer-builders who imaginatively and dramatically used new materials in the most direct manner and with no great sublimation over style. Such was the work of Sir Joseph Paxton, a gardener *cum* engineer, whose crystal palace was an envelope of cast iron and glass. It was designed for the Great Exhibit of 1851 and made a great impression in its day, so much so that it was moved from its first location in Hyde Park to Sydenham, there to stand while the architects went about their own business.

The French also produced engineer-builders who erected remarkable structures for the fairs of 1878 and 1889. Cottancin designed the Galerie des Machines, employing great steel arches over a very wide span, the roof entirely glazed. Gustave Eiffel designed the tower bearing his name, now inseparable from the image of Paris. The French, in the persons of the engineers Hennebeque and Coignet, also invented that contemporary material, concrete reinforced with steel rods.

In America in the same years, the '80s, William LeBaron Jenney and Louis Sullivan were developing the skeleton frame envelope. The latter's department store building for Carson Pirie Scott in Chicago is still a busily used structure. It was in Louis Sullivan's office that Frank Lloyd Wright, the great American original, gathered his early ideas and powers.

The new architecture was developing well under the conception of form growing out of structural needs when a new motivation intruded, esthetics and style. The style was the *art nouveau* most often associated with Aubrey Beardsley and the *Yellow Book* magazine. The style, which caught the esthetic imagination, was mainly involved with the development of a new kind of decoration and ornamentation founded on curved natural forms. It had little significant influence on the architecture that followed. Its main contribution was negative, for it halted the development of the structural rationale which had been going forward. However, none of these experiments in structure or in style was ever strong enough to influence the main body of practicing architects, who continued to produce rich, fashionable and unimaginative buildings in classical styles. None the less, while these rich piles were going up, there were architects working alone and without great recognition. They were pioneering originals—Wright in America, Van de Velde in Northern Europe, Otto Wagner in Vienna—who were later joined by men such as Joseph Hoffman in Austria, H. P. Berlage in Holland, and Peter Behrens in Germany. These dedicated men, working at great odds, were the direct forefathers of modern architecture.

A new and important movement began with the foundation of the Deutcher Werkbund in Germany in 1907. It grew out of the *art nouveau,* but its vitality really came from the attempts to get industry to use the work of modern artists. It was not an art for art's sake movement, but sought applications of modern art to everyday usage. It reached an important goal when Peter Behrens was appointed architect-designer of products for a large German electrical manufacturing company, A.E.G. Behrens' turbine factory of 1909 often is considered Europe's first modern building.

These Middle European developments left most of

the French architects relatively untouched. Their classical education and the tradition imposed by the École des Beaux Arts was firmly entrenched. However, a few French pioneers also were engaged in lonely development. The work of Eugène Freyssenet in his reinforced concrete hangar at Orly in 1916, and particularly the work of Auguste Perret in the same material, is significant. Perret erected a reinforced concrete frame apartment house in Paris as early as 1903 and a striking church in Le Raincy in 1925.

Such was the evolving development of architecture until it ran headlong into French modern painting and sculpture. The transference of inspiration and motivation was not only due to the exciting potential in the new art, but avant-garde society was prepared by experience and temperament for new discoveries in architecture. Cubism had a remarkable effect on architecture. The pure mathematical relationships, the architectonic forms inherent in the paintings when coupled with new structural systems, gave architecture a new face and a new energy. The early work of the great seminal Swiss-French architect Le Corbusier shows this clearly.

As the influence of modern painting and sculpture spread, groups and movements were formed in which architects joined with their fellow artists in developing new theories and approaches. The names of painters and sculptors became linked to those of architects in the development of these new ideas. In Holland a movement known as *De Stijl* was formed. The architect Doesberg was one of its leaders but the painter Piet Mondrian its most persuasive influence. In Russia the constructivist group held, in addition to the architect Malevich, the sculptors Gabo and Pevsner and the painter Kandinsky. In Germany the celebrated Bauhaus at Dessau, the most influential group of all, was headed by the architect Walter Gropius, but also contained the artists Klee, Feininger and, at times, the ubiquitous Kandinsky.

From this period on, modern architecture became conscious of itself as an international movement. The avant-garde architects no longer worked in splendid isolation or in esoteric movements. They were conscious of each other's theories and achievements and were ready with techniques and solutions when social change and economic expansion made the practice possible. So modern architecture came of age. Many gifted men contributed to its formation, but since they were men and artists, the practice of modern architecture reflects individual bents and interests.

Nowicki's threefold base for architecture is not inclusive enough. To humanism, functionalism and construction must be added a fourth, estheticism. Indeed, for the architect, the last today seems the strongest. This has come about for several reasons. Not the least of these is the separation, as mentioned earlier, between the architectural designer and his genie in the bottle, the structural engineer. The latter, the good soldier, makes possible the coming into being of many novel concepts. The architect is left free to practice esthetics while the engineer makes it possible to build. In some instances the designer is the engineer as well. Frank Lloyd Wright's early training as an engineer was of inestimable importance in the development of his designs. Some of the most beautiful constructions in the world are designed by the Italian Pier Luigi Nervi, an engineer. The work of Felix Candella of Mexico shows the same integration of poetically beautiful form and structural logic.

Architectural esthetics are marked by a polarity of taste and belief. One kind of polarity can best be exemplified by the divergence in belief between Le Corbusier and Frank Lloyd Wright. Le Corbusier's writings are full of social ideology coupled with an insistence on functionalism. Yet his recent buildings are neither functional nor do they recognize social and human needs. His apartments at Marseille are anything but reasoned structures growing out of functional use or social need. If in his mind they do meet these, then the needs are less those of men than of his own imaginings. Nevertheless, they are individualistic expressions of a true artist-architect. Le Corbusier's work grew out of the impact of cubism, his work dominated by careful arrangement of concrete forms in an esthetic composition. His more recent work is freer in form, deeper in penetrations and rougher in character of surface. It is a form of abstract expressionism applied to a building.

Frank Lloyd Wright's writings are equally moved by a social ideology which is just as absent in his work. His work was highly personal and he imposed his own geometry on the man who wanted to own one of his buildings, round or hexagonal, as Wright's whim suited. A reminiscence I treasure is one that shows the intransigence and self-assertiveness of Wright. It is that of an exchange between a friend of mine and

F. L. W. The friend, an artist in films, exercised his own esthetic compulsion and designed and built a house for himself. Hearing that Wright was in the neighborhood, he wangled a visit from the master. Wright walked through the friend's house making a running commentary of deprecatory remarks. Finally, in the living room, the capping blow was the complaint that the room was much too high. It did not have human scale, said Wright. The friend, suffering blow after blow to his *amour-propre,* finally drew himself up to his 6 feet 4 inches and allowed that since he was a tall man, and Mr. Wright, conversely short, there must be a justifiable adjustment to human scale. Wright's unhesitating rejoinder was that any man who grew to be more than 5 feet 7 inches was a weed.

Another and perhaps apocryphal anecdote concerns Wright and the Guggenheim Museum for abstract art. This museum is a squat, round edifice containing a spiral ramp which hugs the wall on which the pictures are hung. In the workings of such a ramp museum, those who look at the pictures are processed like so many peas going through a cannery. The flow is one way; very little moving up and back, to and from pictures, is possible. The intent of the structure is to process people through it, not to enable them to look at pictures. If you are to look at anything, look at the building, which, truth to be said, is exciting. It would make a magnificent container for the catafalque of a lost hero, a more functional Les Invalides.

The hanging, lighting and viewing of the pictures in this museum have been a problem from the outset, never quite becoming adequate, even with some of the most intriguing and skillful technical solutions developed by its first curator. Many of these incipient problems were apparent when the building was in plan form. Wright, being asked whether he thought this was the proper kind of building in which to show pictures, is said to have replied, "Have you seen those pictures?"

I use these anecdotes, not to derogate a great artist-architect (if he had done nothing more than "Falling Water" and "Taliesin West" he would have earned a place in history) but to indicate the highly personal approach that Wright had to his art. While in his writings he professed an urgently human motivation and an all-encompassing universality, his architecture was essentially an esthetic and romantic form of self-expression, not overly hampered by human needs. His stylistic doctrine was to identify his structure with the ground flowing line growing out of the earth, but he would often fill these buildings with an artsy-craftsy ornamentation harking back to Ruskin and Morris.

The inescapable fact is that much of contemporary architecture is almost Fascist in concept, if one can use a sociopolitical word to describe a building. As in the case of political despots who present their actions in the most benign human terms, so is much of architectural thinking presented in the most liberal humanistic terms only to impose the most restrictive and obdurate conditions upon the humans who use the buildings.

Both Wright and Le Corbusier are giants of modern architecture, although diametrically opposed in doctrinal concept. Their influence in giving new impetus for search and for freedom in architecture has been enormous, but in recent years the stylistic influence of Gropius and Mies van der Rohe has become more assertive. This can be seen in the rash of new structures which have sprung up all over the world. Their distinguishing hallmark is the glass curtain wall. In the case of van der Rohe, in response to his credo, "less is more," the buildings have been pared to bare essentials—a steel cage with the openings glazed.

The most recent turn of architectural esthetics indicates the growing revolt against the sterile glass cube, perhaps out of boredom, and certainly from the need of younger architects to destroy older idols and replace them with newer credos in their own image. Contemporary sculpture is one of the principal influences. Not that architecture imitates any particular kind of sculpture, but the mixtures of expressionist and constructivist forms extant in modern architecture all can be seen in contemporary sculpture.

Another influential motivation is the intensification in the visible articulation of structural form in an expressionist manner. Each last structural method or member is milked for its ultimate meaning, even to the inclusion of elements which have less structural truth than expressionist conviction. The winning design for the new city hall in Boston, as well as the Fine Arts School at Yale, is that kind of building.

The artist-architect is in his heyday of unrestrained creativity. Man can only mark time and wait for the next turn of the wheel. At that time the motivation for new architecture may turn to his human needs, in the city, in his home and where he works.

Walking on Park Avenue

Park Avenue in New York City is an extraordinary thoroughfare. It is a wide, handsome avenue whose broad prospect is due not so much to the vision of early city planners as to the fact that it was once an open cut that first housed the yards of the New York Central Railroad and later those of the New York, New Haven, and Hartford Railroad as well. It is divided into a northern and southern section by Grand Central Station.

Park Avenue had rather an indifferent beginning. It once started at 34th Street, where, by some feat of legerdemain found usually in European cities, Fourth

Avenue changed into Park Avenue. The northern part of the avenue once was bordered by modest apartments, hotels, houses, clubs and, as it proceeded uptown, a few office buildings. A tunnel runs under the street as the main body of the avenue gradually ascends Murray Hill. The tunnel once housed streetcars, which have since abandoned it to scurrying taxicabs. The tunnel emerges into daylight at 40th Street, where the Renaissance magnificence of Grand Central Station, with the bronze effigy of Commodore Vanderbilt on guard, bursts into view.

The station once dominated the avenue from the south by sitting squarely in its middle. Behind it to the north, thrusting its wedding cake roof into the sky, was the silhouette of the New York Central Tower office building. This building, styled in high Renaissance as befitting a companion set piece for the station, dominated the downtown aspect of Park Avenue. The street circled this New York Central complex of buildings at an upper level, diving back to the regular street level by a steep vehicular ramp which passed through the high arched portals of the tower building. Here it came out on the northern part of the avenue, which was decked over the railroad yards and which, as a matter of fact, still covers the tracks of the present railroad systems. From 46th Street, where it comes out of the portals, it proceeds majestically northward until it disappears into the slum disaster of Harlem. The lower section of this part of Park Avenue once housed some of the most expensive hotels and apartments in New York City.

Such was the quality of the street. But how it has

changed. The station and tower no longer dominate the avenue with their imitation Old World splendor. A huge wall of a building, the Pan Am office building, has been erected between the two. This building not only dwarfs the two older structures, but blots out the silhouetting sky as well. It is faced with a timid version of neobrutalist detail in cast stone. Despite this scaled-down surface design, it seems to bristle like a bully who has moved into a refined neighborhood, and all this despite the fact that these two older buildings were notable for the large scale of their detail.

But this is not the only change. The apartment buildings have folded like the Arab tents and the avenue from 46th to 60th Street now is lined with some of the sleekest new office buildings which have been erected in the United States in the last decade. Among these shining structures are Lever House, the Seagram, Pepsi-Cola, Union Carbide and the Bankers Trust buildings, and just a few intruding commercial versions of the glass cube to give economic realism to this expensive fairyland.

Since my own office is on this part of the avenue, I have been witness to the rising of many of these structures during my daily walks to and from the railroad station and the office. While it is quite true that these buildings go up with breathtaking rapidity in terms of a large structure, nevertheless it takes a little over a year, and a year of constant looking is a long time in terms of one's life. It gives one time to realize them as buildings and as esthetic experiences.

Certainly from the start of construction one is overwhelmed by the engineering marvels which take place right before one's eyes as these structures go up over an operating railway system. Then, as the design solution slowly unfolds, one has ample time to decide on esthetic approval or disapproval. Because of the daily involvement, this approval is not easily given or withheld. There is ample time to consider them. The emerging buildings assume personalities which persist long after they are completed and occupied. There follows a record of two such ruminative experiences.

Night Buildings

In primitive societies, intimate with nature, it was inevitable that inanimate objects would be invested with spirits and deities. Every tree and rock, every structure, had some indwelling spirit. The forest was inhabited by nymphs and goblins. Mountains harbored thunderers. The sea was filled with a host of gods, demigods and strange beasts.

From that midnight forest world to our shiny contemporary buildings is the longest span in man's history. During that leap of time and culture he has discarded bagfuls of beliefs. At this date, to invest the new glistening edifices, the monuments and symbols of our machine age with animism is a most improbable reversion. That sort of folderol was meat and drink for Sir James George Frazer, the Brothers Grimm and Hans Christian Andersen. Now the real nonsleeping midnight world pulses rather with a human pleasure and tragedy. The magic waking-up of clock and toy shops is left for children and balletomanes. Yet I cannot resist the idea that a nonworldly spirit emanates from these buildings at night.

This unlikely venture into metaphysics is rooted in the feeling that these glass buildings are not intended to let light in, but rather to throw light out. During the day all sorts of devices—blinds, drapes and screens —are used inside the glass walls to filter out the overwhelming flood of light. Man is too recently out of the forest to stand so much unrelenting greenhouse sunshine. But at night these crystal edifices stand coldly beautiful, like temples undisturbed by human celebrants, those intruders who destroy the precise relationship through their attempts to adapt the interiors to their mean human frailties. It is at night that the buildings seem to reach their ultimate esthetic purpose. It is then that they glow, perfect and impassive, unmarred by occupants or surroundings. Alas! We are day people and these are night buildings.

The buildings were conceived as enormous hollow sculptures. Human use is incidental to their esthetic purpose, like ants nesting in a towering abstract garden sculpture. It is at night that their lean, skeletal forms best emerge, delineated by the outflowing light. The metal, glass, marble interiors heighten the glow.

In daylight people go through the glass doors, hurry through the metallic interior, and disappear behind the Venetian-blind-enshrouded glass walls. The street-floor areas are empty and sterile. The function of these areas, beyond the fact that they provide a passageway for people from the street to the elevators, is to demonstrate that this great pile of structure is almost separated from the ground. Behold! An enormous cube floating in the air which is balanced on these very few thin columns.

After a sufficient number of buildings have thus been balanced upon their pilotis, one becomes convinced that the feat is entirely possible. But it makes walking up Park Avenue a very barren enterprise. Not all of the new buildings are handsome, but they share one thing in common. We look across one vast empty building lobby after another, peering through the glass shield at the empty stainless steel or marble walls within. Here and there on the avenue are fossil remains of older architecture, archeological landmarks whose premises, while in the process of negotiation for sale to an erector of another glass building, still hold a few show windows. At intervals along the street the eye is bemused by a Rambler automobile, a stuffed tiger nestled against a bottle of Arpege, or a fashionable Cavanagh hat. (As this is being written, the scaffolds are up to tear down one of the buildings.)

Despite the clinical calm of these new buildings, the constant passer-by is aware of ferment going on within. There is indication that a modicum of dissatisfaction exists, at least with the ground-floor premises, in spite of all the admiring assurances that have been heaped upon them. They have been extravagantly praised. Architectural critics from neo-Georgian *cum* Gothic campuses have applauded the clarity and precision of the solutions. Magazines delightedly have published picture after picture. They lend themselves to dramatic black and white compositions, and the lack of intruding architectural detail improves the backgrounds for exotic fashion costumes.

There can be a surfeit even of a lean diet. The unbroken offerings of steel and glass have their limits of appreciation. The building operators have either become aware of some disenchantment or have become bored themselves with looking at their sterile premises, and there has been a gradual change in these empty rooms. The ground floors slowly are turning into exhibition spaces. There is a great competition among buildings to introduce more visually exciting shows in their barren halls. It still is all very institutional and proper.

In one case a most extraordinary, if temporary, transformation took place. It happened in that dreary masonry monument, the Pan Am building. Through its grim lobbies thousands of commuters pour every morning on their way from Grand Central Station to the office buildings to the north. The lobby is a particularly tedious version of contemporary aridity. It is faced with a dark unlovely granite used in contrast to travertine marble. Constructivist murals by Gyorgy Kepes and Josef Albers adorn the upper lobby and a sculpture by Lippold occupies the center of a side lobby. The hall through which the commuters file is of unrelieved dullness, immense, ugly and inhuman.

This last Christmas a lovely thing happened. The building management placed a huge Christmas tree in the central lobby. It was hung with traditional glistening festival decorations. A few presents for needy children were placed under the tree. Suddenly, a flood of presents began to accumulate into a large pile. The architecture of the lobby disappeared. All that was seen was the symbol of human love and gaiety in response to a season of love. The pile of gaily wrapped boxes with their very large labels had the power to make a vast pile of interior masonry disappear and for a brief moment, at least, take on the qualities of human uses and emotion.

With the season of love over, the building returned to its feeling of a stone desert. The brief, lovely experience for the building management must have been very exhilarating and instructive, for now plants in tubs are being placed wherever possible to reintroduce the feeling of man's world. So much for the daytime pleasures in walking up Park Avenue.

But at night there is no need for any agonizing reappraisal. No attempt need then be made to find a human use for space which did not consider humans in the first place. At night the esthetic purpose of the building is clear. The precise relationship of its parts in their strict linearity can be enjoyed like a painting or sculpture. Or, even more farfetched, one can imagine them as stately beauties in some regal court, bedecked in jewels of light, taking their places proudly, awaiting the start of a pavan. There they stand, radiant, waiting for the music to begin—or for daylight, when people start to crawl around again.

These magical changes are not only to be seen on Park Avenue. There are dramatic, isolated instances. The National City Bank branch at Kennedy Airport is such an example. It stands alongside the main approach to the heart of the terminal building complex. The bank building is a chaste and precise glass-enclosed metal cage. It stands on columned legs spaced along its outer perimeter. Access to the upper floor is by a stairway in the center of the covered area. On a normally sunny day, curtains are pulled across the glass to keep out the cruel light. The transparency of the building is gone. It is an opaque glass walled box. At night the change takes place. With the curtains drawn back, the black steel skeleton encloses a brilliantly illuminated crystalline cube. It is empty of people, but the interior glows with a brilliance that lights up the surrounding area; a night-blooming beauty in the vast mechanical garden of Kennedy Airport.

The Wandering Fountains of Seagram

Stories linking beauty with water are a recurring theme in the iconology of fable. We know of the frog who turned into a handsome prince, the ugly and socially misfit duckling who became a beautiful swan, and of Ondine's beauty which destroyed her fisherman lover. These and many other fables are part of the revered heritage of lore which provides us with examples, adages and hope. It is inspiring to see beauty emerge. But with the exception of some sunrises and sunsets at sea, I never had been witness to the gradual emergence of beauty on water.

In the evolution of the fountains at the Seagram building on New York's Park Avenue I have seen such a change. No frog, swan or Ondine this, but the beauty of the play of water. They have turned from precisely measured jets, like the spouts of leviathans lying in some regimented, subaqueous pissoir, to a mass of dancing water which gives pleasure to the eye, the reassurance that the Cinderella myth still lives, and joy in the proof that the techno-mathematical halter which binds us can be broken, and in the breaking bring us fun and delight.

The evolution of the fountains was only a small part of a larger change which has been going on—the change to Park Avenue itself. Once a housing complex for the wealthy, with a rather indifferent architectural character, but exuding the rich aura of success and contentment, a place where fortunate inheritors and clever investors could find peace and plenitude in the company of their peers, the avenue has turned into a crystalline canyon lined with cold and precise people-eating buildings. Not all the buildings are adornments to the avenue. A few are impassively handsome, conceived with a clinical attention to detail so spare that the humans who use them seem to disturb the frozen relationships of the design elements.

One of the handsome ones is Seagram. Brown, bronze and severe, it breathes of expense and technical discipline. In it any sign of carefree human usage would be as jarring as a halloo in a cathedral. People pale into insignificance when you see them through the brown-tinted glass in the lobby. In fact, most times it seems empty of people.

This kind of emptiness is not true of the spacious plaza upon which the building sits. Especially at the lunch period, when the dwellers in the interior recesses of the glass caves from the neighborhood crowd into any open space, straining their faces upward to receive the blessings of the sun. The builders of Seagram splendidly sacrificed the use of a large portion of their street-level property to provide a haven for meridional sun-worshippers. In an additional gracious gesture they sought to adorn the area with a landscape treatment which would enhance the building and bring beauty to the plaza. But, alas, this is where the intruding genie of modern design used his wicked charms.

While it is almost impossible to destroy the value of an open space, especially in areas crowded with buildings, there are degrees of beauty which these open spaces project, especially those which contain pools and fountains. Just to say the words conjures up images of the Rond Point, Concorde, Piazza San Pietro, to think nothing of the beautiful fountains of Versailles or to remind us that Napoleon once called the Piazza San Marco "the world's largest drawing room."

The Seagram building is a particularly rich example of the Miesian Style. The structure was designed by Mies van der Rohe and his associate and then acolyte Philip Johnson. This style began decades ago with a startlingly original and logical arrangement of plan, volume and surface into simple geometric relationships. It provided a basis for a method of design which eventually came to be called the international style. Through the years this style, and especially in the case of Mies, became more concerned with the revelation of the structural bones of a building. Since the structure usually was of steel, and of post and lintel construction, a very strict discipline of vertical and horizontal linear relationship was imposed. As in the case of any linear relationship, a planear architecture grew out which reached a near-final esthetic expression on paper. The emotional effect of the line on paper transferred to the building design can be traced in countless buildings.

This was the esthetic which prevailed when the plaza area was designed. In order to expose the precise linear relationship of the building, the trees were pushed to the rear and sides, out of immediate view. The plaza was treated in the same flat linear esthetic. The results will be enjoyed best by a bird with a taste for this sort of thing who hovers a little north of the flagpole in the plaza, and second best by executives who man the thin brown line of offices that face on Park Avenue.

But from the eye line at plaza level, these linear relationships fall short of the goal of observed beauty which was their intention. To begin with, some of the refinements intended to give scale and interest are hardly seen—such as the borders of the pools themselves. These borders are made up of three descending steps surrounding the pools and going from the plaza level to the floor of the pools. This was not an easy or simple construction process, since the pools are constructed of blocks of stone which had to be precisely set and the joints then endlessly caulked to prevent leakage brought on by the unusual vibration due to the railroad which runs under Park Avenue.

On paper these concentric rectangles which surrounded the indication of the spouts must have made an interesting and strong composition. Unfortunately, when the pools are filled with water, the steps tend to disappear because of the dark color of the stone and the semi-opaqueness of the wind-riffled water. This left the fountains as thin spouts in a flat plane of water almost level with the surface of the plaza, unsupported by any verdure, dimensional sculpture or architectural devices.

As a daily watcher in my walks past, I was aware that my sense of an incomplete esthetic realization was shared by the powers that be of the building. Constant experiments were taking place in an attempt to get more out of what they had. Changes in levels of the water jets were tried when the wind permitted. A high slab building like the Seagram is a great wind sail. It collects the vagrant high breezes and deflects them downward into puffs and vortexes. These breezes would blow spray off the fountains and dampen the passers-by.

Probably in an attempt to overcome this, and perhaps to increase the base of the water spout, new heads for the jets were tried. They threw a mushroom-like spout which, while it did diminish the amount of spray, did not add any scale or beauty—quite the reverse.

There were grim days when no water was there at all, but rubber-booted men brushed off the sunken steps and pool floor and shoveled out the collected debris. At such times the plaza looked like a constructivist theater set, awaiting the start of some stark, unrelenting drama. The descending steps surrounding a series of pipes terminated in the precisely placed sprinkler heads.

This interruption must have put ideas into the heads of disrespectful wags, for one morning the pool was covered with a bilious green froth. Someone had dumped a dye and detergent into the basin.

The search for a more satisfactory solution dragged along for a long time. The spare linearity remained unrelieved and unfulfilling except at Christmas. Then the spareness would give way to pure romanticism. Massed Christmas trees would be arranged in an ascending pyramid, the lower trees at the edges gradually rising to the tallest in the center. The trees were then festooned with a myriad of Christmas lights and the basins filled with water. In a city which prides itself on the beauty of its Christmas displays, while not projecting the same expression of individual participation as in the case of the Christmas tree in the Pan Am lobby, this was one of the handsomest.

Christmas over, the fountains were returned to their measured existence and the vague trials at improvement. One day in my morning march past, I noticed the fountains turned off again and in the midst of the basins, cartoons for what appeared to be a piece of sculpture. They had come in two sizes; medium and the large economy size, one in each basin. It seemed to me at this time that this must be the nadir of hope for doing anything with water.

But one thing you learn while walking on Park Avenue is patience. When I saw nothing else happening, I could only presume (a) that the idea of sculpture had been given up, or (b) that it was going to take a long time to carve.

Another morning as I went by the fountains were on again, but something new had been added. They were still in the same mathematical arrangement, but the shape and texture of the water itself had changed. It was thicker, more irregular, it gushed, it danced.

While the total composition had gained little, the individual jets were more beautiful.

And then one day beauty happened. The linear spell was broken. The plumbers had been called in and the jets massed near the outer end of the rectangular pool. The isolated spouts became a mass of dancing water with volume, life and character of its own. Each spout danced to its own tune but in beautiful concord with its immediate neighbor. The fountains had come into their own—a lovely composition of water, giving off its own mysterious beauty, the result of the free fall, never-quite-repeated play of a mass of water in the air. The fountains, freed from their burden of conforming to a restricting architectural esthetic, had fulfilled their primary purpose.

They have enhanced the plaza, they have brought pleasure and delight to those who see them. Just as in the promise of the fresh green shoot which forces its way up to the sun through a crack in concrete, the evolution of these fountains reassures that with human patience and longing, a way can be found to break through the ever-tightening ring of sterile techno-esthetic forces.

The Concert Hall and the Moonshot Syndrome

Imagine, if you will, the extraordinary life of the citizens of a great city in the wild blue future. In this technical nirvana, activities at work and at pleasure will most likely be regulated by electronic devices, computer-like thinking machines which may even decide who may go to the theater and who may not. There will be no appeal from their decision because it will be known by that time that once programmed, the machines are undeviating in their rectitude.

It is a cold, scary and inhuman prospect. Yet, as an experience, it is not as far distant in the future as you may think, for recently the people of New

York were affected by such a decision. It occurred during the planning phase of the new Philharmonic Concert Hall. Despite the ever-increasing size of the New York musical audience, an electronically conditioned decision was made to replace Carnegie Hall with a smaller hi-fi sort of auditorium, thereby excluding a large segment of the present and yet unborn audiences from sharing a memorable musical experience.

The decisions which shaped the plan of the new hall are the result of the moonshot syndrome, an infection which affects our society in many of its interests and occupations. The infection is rooted in the belief that in this insecure world, truth and integrity can be found only in science and technology. Having once accepted this belief, we necessarily find our greatest affirmations, and therefore the highest order of motivation, in science and technology. The moonshot is the *ne plus ultra* of modern technological achievements. As a motivation and spur it has more potential of imaginative creativity than can be found in the resolution of some constant and nagging human need, and therefore has greater promise of reward for the creator who wishes to leave his indelible mark on the world.

The contemporary artist, architect or designer, in abandoning an old tradition, has logically looked for his motivation to this very popular and modern image. He comes by his direction fairly enough, for in the case of the architect and designer, the work is intimately involved with the techniques of structure and materials. Thus, at one fell swoop, he not only provides himself with a motivation representative of his craft, but is warm and secure in the knowledge that he is a true son of his time. Certainly with such affirmations there can be nothing wrong with the choice of motivation. The unfortunate fact is that it often contravenes the needs and longings of the society in which it works.

The old tradition of a concert hall hardly seems to fit the concept of our modern society, though it still manages somehow to project a warm and charming ambiance, what with its red plush and gilt cupids and the promise of sensuous enjoyment to come. The tradition grew up with the baroque Italian and German princelings. The concert halls were for the private enjoyment of an élite. The public enjoyment of music was restricted to taverns and churches. The élite could not keep such a good thing to themselves for long, and eventually, as public music changed from hymns, cantatas and barroom ballads, it came out of the church and taverns and into the music hall. As the musical audience grew, public halls had to be provided. These first public concert halls were an enlargement of the early private tradition, even to the plush and cupids.

But now we have grown into a modern democratic society, and while the halls perform the same utilitarian purpose, and oddly enough, to a great degree, the same music, we have added a new societal need, the social obligation to provide more for everyone. We do not go at this by halves, even to the training of new musical audiences, for we start the appreciation of music at the elementary school level.

In the case of the new concert hall we have met

this challenge squarely by building a 2,600-seat house to replace a 2,900-seat house. Forgetting the future for the moment, there is a demonstrated need now for a larger house. In Carnegie Hall 500 requests for annual subscriptions for the Philharmonic season were turned down because of lack of space. This does not take into consideration seat sale for individual performances. We therefore have the anomaly of a smaller house in the musical capital of the largest city in the greatest democracy on earth, at a time when our population, and more especially our musical population, is rapidly increasing. In short, in these democratic times, we have built a hall for an élite who can gain admittance.

In addition, the hall is too small to meet the needs of the organizations that use it. The Philharmonic Society, its principal user, is increasingly dependent upon private philanthropy for its means. In this smaller hall they have been denied increased or even equal revenue through ticket sale, making them even more dependent upon the whims of philanthropy. For the moment at least, some sections of our society consider public money for the arts to be a symbol of the softening of our moral fiber or, at the very least, a sign of a swing to Communism.

The orchestra has some alternative choices to add to revenue. They could increase the number of performances or increase the price of the tickets. Neither is a palatable alternative, since the orchestra already gives five performances a week; what with preparation, recording and program making, this is considered to be an optimum number. The idea of the new hall was vigorously sold to the public, for there was a surprisingly successful movement to save old Carnegie. In the face of such an unwarranted display of affection on the part of a considerable number of people for the discarded temple of music, a significant price rise would perhaps be unpopular, to say nothing of the fact that such a price rise is not in the public interest, as it might exclude people for a more undemocratic reason than just not having a seat. A larger audience can be reached by broadcasting, but the main purpose of a hall is to create empathy and contact between art, artists and the public. Too much of esthetic enjoyment has been reduced to a mechanistic and unshared experience.

So much for the compelling reasons for a larger house. How did the decision to build a smaller hall come about? In abandoning the old tradition as being unrepresentative of a modern society, it naturally leaves the problem of replacement up to a new direction or motivation. It is easy enough to change the appearance; for that matter, many new and exciting architectures are in the process of evolution. But is that enough? The men in charge of the planning were and are men of integrity and not entirely in the fashion business. Though it is difficult to recognize the fact by what we see around us, we are assured that style is not a large enough motivation for architecture today. This is where the moonshot syndrome comes in.

In motivating a concert hall, two popular technical developments are at hand—the attractive new packaged appliance containing certain electronic equipment called the hi-fi set as a motivation for looks, and the (absolute?) science of acoustics for goals. The questioned qualifier is my own. For while sound is subject to accurate measurement, it is also subject, in musical considerations, to personal taste. A musical sound can be dry, brittle or shrill, or it can be soft, mellow or mushy. The quality of sound can emphasize the low tenebrous tones of the deep-voiced instruments, or it can reinforce the shriller voices of the higher-pitched instruments.

It is a matter of record that the public and its experts have swung in taste from one quality to another in the span of years. We have only to remember the high esteem given recordings of Bach played by Stokowski several years ago and how this esteem has slipped in the face of recent interpretations. A drier, more acrid sound is popular today. In one area of acoustical requirement there can be little question or challenge—the same quality of sound must, if possible, be heard in all parts of the hall. The questioned area lies rather with the kind of sound that is being pitched to an organ as inexact as the human ear.

Within reason a fine degree of excellence can be achieved in a hall if care is taken in its design. But in the new concert hall, in response to the moonshot syndrome, the desire was to create an acoustic quality rivaling or exceeding anything anywhere in the world. This implies a level of excellence that begins to reach ranges inaudible to the human ear. The task for the human sonar system to isolate and identify this excellence is like trying to give exact qualitative and quantitative ratings to words used in consumer advertising, words such as prime as against choice, or giant as against super.

The ground was prepared for the workings of the syndrome by the state of musical appreciation itself. There has been a gradual shift in the kinds of emphasis in the appreciation of music. Starting with the era in which the composer was the center and hero of musical experience, the emphasis gradually shifted from the content of Bach, Mozart, Beethoven, to performance, and connoisseurs treasured remembered performances and recordings of Heifetz, Horowitz and Toscanini.

The interpreter is still the hero, but a new set of values is emerging—the electronic transmission of sound. Countless numbers huddle over the oscilloscope of their hi-fi units, watching the balance of the stereo sound as it flows from their twin batteries of tweeter, woofer *et al.,* proud of the performance of the machine which can produce sounds which they cannot hear but their dog can. So the quality of sound is taking its place alongside of interpreter and content in the scale of values.

Therefore, since the science of acoustics was necessarily the principal source for motivation in planning, the next part of the problem was how to apply it. There are few great bodies of correlated empirical research in existence. Guidelines for the acoustic solutions must be developed, not subjectively, but scientifically. So the engineers and the scientists sallied forth, armed with a battery of electrical gadgets. In my mind's eye I can picture these earnest men with their little black boxes furnished with little black needles which twitched at a sound. All over the Western world orchestras and artists poured out the music of Bach, Beethoven and Stockhausen to ap-plauding audiences, also to the anonymous little black boxes whose needles coldly registered reverberation and decibels and God knows what besides.

These are no wild enthusiasts, these little black boxes. They are not moved by a Heifetz or an Oistrakh. They don't even quiver when Glenn Gould scratches him-self in the middle of his Sunday afternoon. No; they simply, dedicatedly and implacably measure and re-measure, and when the facts are in, lay down the rule. In any audience which exceeds 2,000, there is a de-terioration in sound as the number goes up. The Black Oracle has spoken and the people accept The Judg-ment. Stop having children! There's no room at the inn. We are sold out.

There was a harsh decision to be made. Should the choice be a larger hall which would take care of an expanding audience with good acoustics (recent prece-dents for this exist, one being London's new Royal Fes-tival Hall, which seats 3,600) or should the choice be a hall that could outrival any hall in existence in the scientific quality of its sound? The mandarins, respond-ing to the moonshot syndrome, unhesitatingly chose the latter. The die was cast, it would be a smaller hall.

When the first plans were exposed, there was an outcry—not from the public. What do they know? It came from the concert managers. These people know. They sell tickets. They pay artists. So in response, the house count was raised, but not even equal to old Carnegie. The little black boxes wouldn't like that.

The decision was more important than a choice between a thrill for the *cognoscenti* with a hall that has a longer reverberation time than the Vienna Grosser Musikvereinssaal, as against providing good facilities for the deserving more. What is at stake here is the whole question of values by which we conduct the business of living. Is our awe of technical achievement so great that it begins to have a purpose of its own separated from man, or is man still the center of his own universe? Is he doomed to come out second best whenever the decision is to be made between the best of all possible mechanical worlds and himself? When a compromise must be made, why is it he who must give way? There does not seem to be any safeguard in the obvious fact that men make their own technical decisions. Man, the creator, seems to have a motivation of his own.

The monstrous joke is that on September 23, 1962, the hall opened with great fanfare and advance propaganda of the care taken with the acoustics. To a man, the critics and public complained of the quality of the sound. It was a hi-fi set that simply would not hi-fi. The engineers are still tuning the hall like a balky ukelele. They may yet enable the hall to rank acoustically with the first in the world. Or maybe the little black boxes were wrong.

The American House—
Art Object or
Human Experience?

The contemporary American house is like the animal that was put together by a committee. It reflects the differing interests, attitudes and imperatives found in any group undertaking. Not that the house is, in fact, a product of any concerted single action by a group. Rather, it is a result of years of evolvement under the pressures of individual interests.

In recent years the pace of change has increased. Like other kinds of architecture, the house is the result of a rapidly changing technology and the acceptance of a new esthetic. More immediately, however, the house reflects the impact of the population explosion, the decentralization of living centers and an expanded economy. The groups and agencies who have influenced the house, the animal committee as it were, are the tract builders, the lending agencies, the building materials manufacturers and, to a lesser degree, the artist-architects. These all have affected the houses of a cowed public whose inborn desires still are shaped by a building tradition incompatible with a modern society.

My concern in this book is the chasm between contemporary esthetics and man. It would therefore seem a far cry to discuss anything as banal as the American house. And yet, in the area of architecture, how can anything so affecting the lives of people as does the house not be discussed?

In addition, present imperatives place great importance upon esthetics, and the architects, as they are doing in the rest of architecture, are exploring avenues of stylistic expression rather than of human need. Therefore, while the appearance is quite radically different, the motivation is not unlike that which produced the early 20th-century version of the carpenter Gothic house. There are obvious failures for humans in the house. It does not meet the needs of a family in the present society. A concentration upon avant-garde esthetics will do little to improve the house as a living unit. It has been my point throughout that both the artist and man would be enriched if the artist would find the sources for his creative motivation through the needs of man in a modern society rather than wallowing in borrowed esthetics.

A point of further clarification at the outset. While

a line must be drawn between the avant-garde house and those in which most Americans live, the failures in both spring from the same sources. The greatest amount of exploration, and certainly of esthetic license, occurs in the avant-garde house. However, the people who live in them obviously are ready to make the sacrifice necessary in terms of living for the pleasures of esthetics or of status derived through ownership of something way-out. In addition, they are the people who can afford the expense and effort it requires to alleviate the obvious failures by one improvisation or another. Therefore, while a tract house and a modern custom-built house may be radically different in appearance, they still suffer from the same basic failure—the motivations which affect the design grow from elements more often outside human need than in its recognition—although the needs of the avant-garde customer have other kinds of status requirements and the means to indulge them.

The concept of need has been altered. When a man talks about needs in a home today he is not speaking of elementary fears that his wife and children may be exposed to the weather or sickness, or be terrorized by ravening beasts. What he calls "need" is in part need for self-improvement, self-statement, self-establishment. Nor are these needs less real or less admirable than others. His desires for well-being, comfort, position among his fellows, beauty, grace and spiritual reward are as real as his physical requirements.

A rather startling statistic indicates a glaring failure in the house. One out of every five Americans moves every year. While unquestionably some of these moves are a sort of enforced migration due to change of employment, by far the greatest percentage of those who move do so for other reasons. In a study by Dr. Peter Rossi of the University of Chicago[1] on why people move, he lists the reasons given in order of their priority. The first three reasons were concerned with the inadequacy of the house. A principal reason is that while the family unit is dynamic, the house is not. While the family expands or contracts, the house is a frozen unit of containment which can be changed only with a great deal of attendant trouble and expense, if at all.

In earlier times the family accommodated itself to its housing. In the present state of an expanded economy, people are less willing to make that accommodation. If a house is too small, they refuse to be cramped. The doubling up in sleeping rooms which was customary in bygone days no longer seems to be a palatable solution. Increased income and expanded credit facilities make moving possible. Increased income and its resulting status requirements are an additional reason behind so much moving. While we are not a classless society, it is possible for a man to move rapidly upward in the various layers of class since these class lines are largely a result of stratification at various income levels. We are blessed with great social mobility as the direct effect of our ability to increase income, that is, if no religious or racial barriers exist.

The character of our newer communities is a stereo-

[1]*Why People Move* (Glencoe: Free Press of Glencoe, 1950).

type of the same kind of house and of parallel income levels. The houses and the people in them take on a mass packaged look; nevertheless, these very communities are the roots of young married people in what is called the family-formation period. As these families mature and their incomes increase, the natural desire to keep their roots is overcome by the need to reflect their new status. They move. As a result, we have a "lonely crowd" of people milling about in impersonal space in unfamiliar neighborhoods. It is the inadequacy of the house as a people-container and the failure of the community to hold onto people which brings about so much of the migration. The social implications in such mass uprootings are disquieting.

The family is the central social unit in a stable society. Few things are as important to the family as their home. It is the center and focus of their life, the setting for the events of their collective human existence. It is the repository of all the family's joint and individual memories, its possessions and memorabilia. It is an essential physical ingredient in the cohesive which keeps a family together.

It is a tragedy for the individual, for the family, indeed for society, when people are forced to uproot themselves. For implicit in that uprooting is the separation from place. A home is a unit which exists in a finite relationship to place. Belonging to a place is a central concept which runs through man's history, art and poetry. He is from Devonshire, Brittany, Boston or Dallas. A man is identified with his land, his community, his neighborhood, its institutions and customs. It is part of his dress and his attitudes.

There is a double consequence in this enforced diaspora, for while the uprooting from the community affects the family, the loss of the family affects the community as well. What remains is a deadly, monotonous stereotype of income, attitude and environment. An essential to a dynamic community is its ability to hold families of a range of fortunes and sizes. In its needs for a differing mixture of types of humans it calls for differing types of houses, sites and landscaping character. The success of the community eventually reposes in the success of the individual house. If we are to create a social condition wherein people have roots in a community in which the mix of personality, age and fortune enriches each individual, the ability to remain in the house must be reinforced.

The unequal dynamism of house and family is a first cause. The average length of occupancy in the newer houses is seven years. In a moonshot response to this problem it is not unreasonable at our present level of technology to think of an expandable house. For that matter, it is entirely consistent with thinking which goes on in industry. No business moves into new quarters without consideration and provision for expansion against its projected future. But if a business is expected to grow, nothing is surer than the fluctuation in family size. The house is designed as though no child is born, no one dies, no one joins the family, no one grows up. It is as though the family were a fixed unit in time and in taste, in members, in functional and esthetic characteristics. Scant attention in the design of the house is paid to the phenomena of change. It seems important, therefore, to conceive of the home as a flexible living unit rather than a frozen solution. At hand are many techniques of modular structural systems and of manufactured components.

Components which essentially are factory-assembled units of bathroom, storage and sleeping facilities can give promise for great improvement in the future. The present house still is being assembled on the site, laboriously and expensively, of bits and pieces of building materials, exactly as it has been for centuries. In conception it has not changed for centuries. It still is a large box containing a series of smaller boxes. These inner boxes are all the same except as to size—some are larger than others—and yet the human functions that go on inside them are vastly different. Entertainment, conversation and play, cooking and eating, bathing, all are precise and separate human functions. People at times are ill, or must study and learn. Yet the only major change that has taken place in the last several decades is the moving indoors of the toilet room and the installing of interior climate control.

The bathroom is one of the smaller boxes. It is furnished with leakproof porcelain furniture, all contained in a leaky room, which contributes disaster to neighboring rooms in the form of falling plaster, shredded wall paper, stained walls and mildew. It is technologically possible to achieve—indeed experimental units have been tried—a component bathroom which is totally leakproof. These can be washed and scrubbed to meet the highest requirements of sani-

tation. Such a room, moreover, is integrated with its
own plumbing so that, if needed, the bathroom can
be moved to a new location in the expanded house.
Its individual water and heating systems can be tied
onto the central systems by an umbilical cord of
piping. The new plastic materials lend themselves to
great variations of treatment in color and texture,
giving new basis for decoration. These suggestions
certainly are not offered as a design solution; rather
they are an indication that the design of a home
could start with entirely new thinking. We can face
the challenge of meeting human needs with a new
and available technology instead of constant variations on an old and tired esthetic theme.

The same is true in quite another area of the
house. Consider the bodily function of sleep. In our
tension-ridden society we have built large industries
around sleeping pills, tranquilizers, eye masks, ear
plugs *et al.,* and yet in the consideration of the sleeping room we are satisfied with building a medium-
sized box and equipping it with a bed. There are
certain physical qualities that aid or hinder sleep
—the elimination of noise from within and without
the house, the control of light through the windows,
the control of ventilation. The TV manufacturer
enables us to lie in bed all snug and warm and by
pressing a button to change the channel or shut off
the instrument without getting out of bed, but we
must scurry across the cold floor to shut the window
in the morning or to close it against sudden storm
or rain. The TV control may be a gadget, yet it is
interesting to note the amount of ingenuity which

goes into the increased sale of appliances and the stagnant approach to the solution of such an important human problem as sleep.

Instead of so much concentration of styling the house in fashion's *dernier cri,* the research and development of individual environments and spaces for important bodily functions can unquestionably engender new forms which in themselves create a basis for a new and vital esthetic. The house today is being studied either as a product for sale or as a piece of sculpture for the magazines. As a product it is filled with gimmicky appliances which are endless repetitions of themselves. In several decades the old coal or wood cooking range has undergone fission. The house which once contained a single cooking unit, the stove, now proudly can boast of a multitude of cooking units. Nearly every pot has its own cooking unit attached. We have coffeemakers, potato fryers, toasters, bean pots, skillets, roasters, broilers, kettles and so on into the electrically lighted night. We have taken the old set of living boxes and filled them with a multitude of machines for cooking and cleaning and for adjusting the temperature and humidity. We have been inventive and successful in turning the house into a product.

In the pursuit of esthetics we have been equally inventive, but not quite as successful. The house was first shorn of its roof, then it was put back on in a quick turnabout. A series of excessive gables, butterfly shapes and arcs, shells and vaults have been tried. The house has been placed on pilotis or cantilevered from stone walls. The wall penetrations were enlarged and larger windows inserted. Finally, the opaque walls were done away with entirely, and the windows became the walls. The window wall is the esthetic order of the day. What started out as an admirable attempt at brightening dark interiors now has become a problem of glare and light and heat control.

Because of the urgency of a ruling style, the problems have had only halfhearted attempts at solution. But lo! The glass industry is about to solve the problem which their material has created. They are developing glass with a lower level of light transmission. In other words, the glass is losing a degree of its transparency. Somehow or other this whole progression seems ludicrous. First is the architects' commendable desire to "let there be light." Then glass becomes a style and the glass window takes over the whole exterior wall. But since so much light and glare is hard to live with, the glassmakers start to make the glass increasingly opaque. The impetus of fashion does not permit going back to other old-fashioned opaque materials. There must be uproarious laughter in the glassmakers' heaven.

The shelter magazines (the name generally given to those publications devoted to news and advertising of homes) need sensation to keep themselves lively and up-to-the-minute. The kind of houses which get preferential treatment by these magazines follow that sort of mandate. They must be lively and up-to-the-minute. The result is that the houses we see most often published, which therefore are acknowledged to be the image of preferred housing, seem to be built for people who never grow old or are never ill. The idea of being ill in one of these fashionable show-cases would be an affront to the artist-architects who conceived them. And yet, we do grow older, and as we do, it does not seem too much to expect that the house will recognize that our step becomes less firm and that we cannot reach as high, or that we will need more coddling and comforting.

The cowardly new world plan to banish our aging citizens to a necropolis called a retirement center is a ghastly and inhuman way of solving the problems of accommodating older citizens in housing. Our inability to provide communities that can hold and retain a cross section of age levels also is at fault. Aging citizens have as profound a love for life as do the younger ones. To be segregated and buried alive while still breathing seems an indecency masquerading as planning. I have seen a group of beaming elders crowded around a perambulator which had been propelled into a retirement area during a casual morning walk. It was a moving experience to see these people bunched around the child, the innocent symbol of life, and to be aware of their happiness in seeing it.

Unquestionably there is a pull of softer climates on those who have withstood the rigors of Northern weather for most of their lives, but curiously, in the apartment houses which are going up like a rash across the country at the present time, there has been a surprisingly high percentage of retirement-aged people who have rented space. They do not wish to leave the place with which they have identified their lives, nor the associations and institutions which they have enjoyed over the years.

The house has been studied as a product and as a technical problem. The house has been studied as an art object. It is time to study the house in terms of people in a modern society.

So much for the house itself. The other great failure is the house in relation to the land. Many of our problems today are created by antiquated codes and zoning ordinances, but probably the greatest source of our problem is our tradition in the use of land. We have inherited the English tradition of housing as differentiated, say, from the Mediterranean or Oriental traditions.

In the English tradition the house is located on its own individual site. The Englishman's home is his castle and so is the American's split-level ranch house. The disastrous result of the continuation of this tradition is seen in the sprawling monotonies we call tract developments. Each mirror-image house sits on its own postage-stamp plot. It is an ugly stereotype which is the epitome of depersonalization. The tradition extends to those multiples of living called row houses, where, despite the fact that they are attached, they still remain individual, if repetitious. They still project the same quality of depersonalization. The English in their better examples, however, were able to salvage some quality, as they did in Belgrave Square and other squares of similar concept. In these the quality of the integrated landscape treatment of the square, coupled with the Georgian composition of the whole complex, creates an intimate grouping.

In the Mediterranean tradition the house is not hung

out there for everyone to see and measure. It is hidden behind a common street wall. This wall is an egalitarian device which turns life inward, into courts and patios. There is no denying that this kind of housing has produced as much squalor as have other forms, but the squalor is the result of poverty rather than of a housing method.

An Oriental tradition of housing, particularly in some Japanese examples, is basically the placement of dwelling units on the land in compounds. In its better examples it has resulted in a magnificent integration of small landscape areas with the dwelling units. Despite its multiple-dwelling nature, great privacy can be afforded to the individual units of a family group because the land and building are composed in a manner integrated for the use of people rather than as a single structural composition. Thus, within one building, families can live private inward existences in both the house and intimate landscape area and still be part of a communal enjoyment of the larger entity. This kind of housing is a direct reflection of the tribal or family clan social organism. Unfortunately, most of the Orient is hagridden by poverty, and the instances of such examples of housing are rarely seen, except in the cases of large estates or the richer family complexes. Still, the arrangement holds lessons for those who wish to examine other methods of organized dwellings.

There is considerable thinking going on today in new approaches to land use. Cluster plans, community enclaves and new analyses of multiple dwellings are undergoing tentative experiments. In some enlightened instances, social and behavioral scientists are working with the land planners and developers. The problem thus is being attacked from a concerted social and economic aspect. This can afford the truest bases for an esthetic solution. All approaches must be made together. When the artist-architect sneers at economics, he simply is imitating the painter-sculptor kind of artist who has assumed no stake in society other than his own well-being.

In the case of housing, esthetics, economics and social need are inextricably intertwined. More than that, economics and social need can be the springboard for a new platform for esthetics. Esthetics must not be concentrated entirely upon the idea that the house, the container of living experience, is simply an exploration of the kind of sculpture to which we can adapt ourselves, be it circular or polygonal. Nor that esthetics begin and end with myriad ways of demonstrating that the post really meets the lintel. Nor that since now it is possible to build a transparent cage, this, too, is a kind of life experience to which we must find an accommodation for ourselves.

The new esthetics could spring from the human being with his human problems as the first necessity. This is truer in the house than in any other area of the artist's endeavor.

Part **4**

Communication in Art

"I believe only in French culture and I regard everything else in Europe as a misunderstanding," spake Friedrich Nietzsche, certainly not a man given to temperate ideas, nor one who permitted much latitude in acceptance of his judgments. He was not offering an idea for consideration. He asked for commitment.

Contemporary art asks for the same measure of commitment and belief. To experience the truth of contemporary art as it is presented to us, we must accept the principle that ideas can exist in form alone; that the content of a picture does not necessarily need any identification with human experience other than that which the observer subjectively brings to it, and that the idea of the picture is its form and color. Everything else is a misunderstanding.

Against this narrowed spectrum of consideration is the art of the past, in which form and idea, directly related to human experience, exist separately and conjointly. Together they make content. When these two exist in equilibrium, we have a communicative esthetic statement. The idea of such equilibrium has been a central concept in art for ages. Aristotle spoke of this unity as a final cause. To him the purpose of art was to capture the essence of things through the unity of a representation of life set down in a form which recognized the cooperation and symmetry of all the parts of the whole. The accomplishment of this unity would arouse the profoundest feelings and emotions in those who contemplated such an art. It was the mark of a civilization to provide the soul with works worthy of such contemplation.

Now, when faced with the totality of art, the art of the past and the art of the present, the appreciator must adopt two different attitudes. In his appreciation of the art of the past he employs both of his faculties, of understanding and of feeling. He calls on his conscious and subconscious experiences and on his esthetic responses. In the contemporary art, on the other hand, he relies mainly on his sensate reactions, his subconscious and esthetic responses. He has no conscious relationship through experience and little understanding. Nowhere is the cleavage between the past and present as clearly defined as in the aspect of art called communication.

To Tolstoy, art was the means of communication of emotion. For the Dutch modernist painter Piet Mondrian, such an externality as emotion and communication imposed on the inner considerations of form disturbed the true reality. In Tolstoy and Mondrian (although they practiced different arts) we find opposing extremes in the beliefs that mark the polarities operative in artistic motivation.

Between these two beliefs lies an enormous range of speculative choice. It is evident from the history of art that the artist has found sufficient motivation for his personal creativity in every variation of that choice. It also is evident that as art has progressively become involved with purely technical considerations, a greater chasm has opened up between art and ordinary man. The heart of the reason for the split lies in the communicability or noncommunicability of contemporary art. As art has become more incomprehensible, the ordinary man has felt shunted aside and rejected.

The late Spanish philosopher Ortega y Gasset wrote, "If a man dislikes a work of art but understands it, he feels superior. If, on the other hand, he dislikes a work of art but does not understand it, he is humiliated and angry. Through an act of incomprehensibility, the work of art has compelled the average citizen to realize that he is incapable of receiving the sacrament of art and is blind and deaf to pure beauty. The mass of man, accustomed to ruling supreme, feels that an art for the privileged aristocracy of the finer senses endangers their rights as men."

The problem of communication is, of course, the

timeless problem of art. The poet Horace advised the artist, "If you want me to weep, you must first grieve." Horace touched the very essence of communication, for if the artist is to evoke a response to his grief, joy or anger, he must convey his emotions in comprehensible language. That language may be complex; understanding may require that the audience learn a new language, have shared an experience, have some subconscious identification with the artist's experience. All this the artist can ask of his audience, for communication places requirements on both the artist and his public.

But communication, to take place, must start at the source with the desire to communicate. This desire cannot honestly be said to exist in art today. For the contemporary artist, driven by a search for his own individuality, and enjoying the libertinage of an art that knows few restraints, has turned to technique and inward self-searching rather than to the communicative characteristics of art. Where, before, a work of art operated under the double discipline of form and communication, with form serving as a vehicle of communication, now the artist has abandoned the discipline or even desire for communication in order to give greater freedom to his exploration of form.

With one element of content removed, idea, the work becomes less comprehensible. Understanding is limited to a subjective response, different perhaps for each observer. Any relationship between the artist and observer through the work is based on a trained appreciation of the technical qualities or wholly reliant on a sensate reaction.

Sensate response always has been present in art. No individual really has a clean slate upon which to record response. No one is completely free of experience, and it would require a vacant mind to be free of all prejudice. Most visual works in the graphic and plastic categories have a basis for meaning, since the observer cannot help relating them to some experience of his own, or identifying them with some real object he either has seen or imagined. Sensate reaction is only one of the means by which communication is established. It is present in all of the major systems through which the visual arts have communicated. These can be broadly categorized as naturalism, formalism and symbolism. The same general sort of devices as a basis for communication can be found in writing and in the performing arts.

In painting, naturalism is the most direct means. It embraces all those representations of recognizable objects—trees, clouds, the beauty of women—all of the things of our seen world which provide the onlooker with instantaneous recognition and conscious experience. This is the simplest form of the mechanics of naturalism. More importantly, the artist in this kind of painting communicates his individual vision of nature. The impressions made upon us by some paintings are so strong that we reconstitute a scene in our visible world in the artist's terms. When we have become sufficiently aware of an artist's work it would be difficult to look up a narrow street in Montmartre toward the white dome of Sacre Cœur without subsconsciously composing it as Utrillo did, or to witness a sunset at sea and not see it through Turner's eyes.

There is a delightful story of Whistler and his passion for painting the Thames which points up this effect of the reshaping of our visual world by the artist. At a gallery a woman came up to Whistler and said that she had come to the show on a bus along the Thames. "It was a whole series of Whistler paintings," she exclaimed. "Yes, Madame," Whistler replied, "nature is creeping up."

In novels and plays naturalism, more often called realism, is the device which uses an immediately recognizable life situation to recall parallel experiences in the reader or audience in order to heighten emotional participation in the work. Dialogue holding the rhythms and ideas of ordinary speech increases the sense of realism, as does the use of recognizable place names, enabling us to identify with the work at hand. Everyone probably remembers an incident which illustrates the degree of involvement on the part of an audience in the theater. Tears and cries of fear are commonplace. But along with the tales of fierce Westerners who, from the audience, have taken a shot at the menacing villain is my memory of a young friend at a Christmas children's performance. With a struggling Robin Hood held face-to-face with the venomous Sheriff of Nottingham, my dauntless young friend, a son of a college professor, stood up in his seat and shouted "Kick him in the balls, Robin Hood!" to the consternation of the shepherding adults, the cheers of his peers and the embarrassed tears of his mother. Emotional involvement in a realistic presentation operates at all ages and levels.

Naturalism can even make works of an improbable or imaginary character seem real. A most memorable occasion of this kind was the Orson Welles radio play about a Martian invasion aired on October 30, 1938. The techniques employed were so realistically perfect that a large number of listeners were frightened into actions ranging from calls to the police for advice to actual flight from the threatened danger.

Formalism, another means of communication, in simplified terms is a visual narrative method by which the artist conveys an image of something never seen, but which strikes a chord of response in man's heritage, history, allegory, literature. The quality of this kind of response in painting depends upon the knowledge and experience of the perceiver. In this means of communication we also have established for us a recognizable image never seen in life but easily identifiable.

Outside of paintings, book illustrations or a Chinese New Year's parade, it can safely be presumed that no one has ever seen a dragon. Yet a child can describe one, even to the smoke from its nostrils. The dragon is an example of allegorical iconography by which artists of succeeding generations borrow images from former ones.

Historical poses and relationships are established which have consistent meanings. To most Americans, a man in Revolutionary costume, standing, one knee cocked up, while being rowed across an ice-choked river, can be no one else than Washington crossing the Delaware. In the same vein a man wearing a cocked hat, his hand tucked into his coat at the chest, can be no one but Napoleon. Three nude females posed in a circle or with arms interlocking generally are the three Graces. The Garden of Eden has been illustrated by a nude male and female figure standing on either side of a fruit-bearing tree, or by a serpent, with or without the human figures, coiled around the trunk, bearing an apple in his mouth. If it is simply the depiction of an apple tree without the suggestion of the historical pose or relationships, it can hold any number of bucolic meanings. Artists generations apart, from Giorgione to Titian to Ingres, etc., have identified the sensuous beauty of women in the pose of the sleeping Venus.

Formalism is a device long present in the performing arts. Mythological, historical or classical characters and events have been used as a vehicle to examine contemporary problems or attitudes by dramatists from Euripides and Sophocles to Shakespeare and Racine and on to O'Neill and Anouilh. The tales and legends are so well established as to become archetypal, the story so well known that the dramatist need spend little time on mere exposition to establish his plot line. He can compress that part of his storytelling. His auditor fills in the gaps from his own informed background. This gives the dramatist greater opportunity to focus on his version or aspect with concentrated power. The archetypal character of the story lends itself to varied interpretation with meanings inherent beyond direct translation. The story therefore becomes an excellent carrier for a contemporary comment. It can supply the basis of understanding for a very complicated means of expression. It becomes a carrier for an art form which would have difficulty under other circumstances.

In his music drama *Tristan and Isolde,* Wagner uses the legend of Tristram and Yseult to create a work of sensual beauty throbbing with the pain and glory of love. Opera as a form does not readily lend itself to any realistic treatment of story material. The necessity to deliver arias or to provide opportunity for the chorus and orchestra to fill in interludes or establish mood distorts the human action, making it static and unnatural.

In *Tristan,* Wagner stretches the time sequence of normal human actions to extraordinary lengths in order to accomplish his musical aims. Despite the unnatural posturing into which his principals are forced, the audience cannot escape emotional involvement with the tragic pair. Wagner uses this formalistic device to create a work of great artistic beauty. Yet the story holds no surprises. It is simply a vehicle for his music; the orchestra and the singers' voices are the elements which awaken the responses to a work of overwhelming power. There is no subconscious desire to have the story move along, to see how it comes out. Instead, because this is known, the audience surrenders itself to the music.

Curiously, in a mood of militant anti-Wagnerism, Debussy set out to use the same kind of story, this time that of Pelléas and Mélisande, again to convey a comment upon tragic love. Instead of the clamor and pathos of Wagner, Debussy set himself the task of telling a known love story in terms of quiet resignation and beauty. He almost carried it off. Unfortunately, it is difficult to create and sustain a mood of tragic love in such consistently restrained terms. But again, his near masterwork was made possible by the formalistic approach to his task of communication.

Ballet also uses the same kind of device. The movements of a ballet dancer are extremely conventionalized and executed within a strict form. In the classical ballet especially, the form is restrained to peripheral movement as against the broader central movement of the modern dancer. Leaps and turns start and end with well-established positions and attitudes. Within such a restricted and disciplined framework of movement it is difficult to communicate anything but the broadest suggestions of emotion. When a story line is used, it is stretched beyond the normal length useful to communicate a sustained emotion. Nevertheless, the pre-established knowledge of the story enables the audience to interpret the dancer's movement in terms of what the dancer wished to communicate. Since the story generally is well known, there is neither an overwhelming intrusion of plot nor the straining to understand. The audience is left relatively free to enjoy its own response to kinetic loveliness and interpretation. It is a double use of formalism—both by content and by means.

Another multiple usage of formalism occurs when succeeding generations use the same tale or legend which has been established in man's heritage of story and adapt it to their own needs. The tale of Troilus and Cressida was an invention that grew out of Homeric legends. In English, before Shakespeare, its best-known version was by Chaucer. Shakespeare, it is thought by some commentators, was moved to write his version when the situation between Essex, Southampton, Cuff and the Queen and her ministers seemed to hold a parallel with the situation in the play in which Achilles, Patroclus and Thersites are at odds with Agamemnon, Nestor, Menelaus and Ajax. These commentators believe that Shakespeare saw a remarkable similarity and, to suit his own ends, used it.

Whether this scholarly interpretation is right or not, *Troilus and Cressida* remains one of Shakespeare's most puzzling plays. It is filled with cynicism and bitterness. Love and heroism are both denigrated. When it is played in the costume and period of the *Iliad* it is difficult to make the transference from the ethos and heroism one usually identifies with that glorious epic and time to the disillusionment and lack of honor implicit in Shakespeare's play.

I have seen it twice. Once it was played for all of its comical qualities, for its laughs and French bedroom farcical potential. It did not seem like Shakespeare nor like any of the heroes I knew. Then it was my good fortune to see a production of the play in which Agamemnon, Menelaus, Ajax *et al.* were cast as Prussian generals wearing the uniforms of World War I, replete with spiked helmets and monocles. The meaning and intention became crystal clear, even if the Homeric heroes were not quite the kind I remembered. I had brought to this production a set of conditioned attitudes that made possible the transference from another formulated set of ideals. By a brilliant formalistic device, the production of the play was able to convey the exact intention of a great playwright.

Formalism has great communicative strength because the emotions already have been channeled and directed by past experience. Anything which parallels that original emotion heightens the impact.

A third major element of communication calls into play a symbolical or intuitive range of perception. Here comprehension requires identification of a symbol. In Western civilization the cross symbolizes Christianity, a halo indicates saintliness. The identities of particular saints and martyrs are pictorially established by the use of symbols associated with them. A lion at his feet marks St. Jerome, carnal visions imply St. Anthony; a child on his shoulder while fording a stream, St. Christopher.

Some symbols have come to have a universal meaning. The dove and olive branch have come to be symbols of peace. Despite its origins as an early totem symbol, the swastika in our time has become identified with Nazism. As a symbol it immediately recalls a whole set of social and political attitudes. Architectural monuments are symbolic of places. The Eiffel Tower means Paris; the Houses of Parliament, London; St. Peter's, Rome; the pyramids, Egypt, etc. These are examples of the direct use of symbols.

The use of symbols in art also includes that area of human understanding in which the symbols stimulate an analogous though not directly recognizable experience. In symbolic painting the sensual, emotional and intellectual capacities combine to evoke a subjective response through association, color or form. Such a response stems either from a primitive, instinctive surrender to the emotions aroused by the symbol, or from an accurate knowledge of the symbols, their implication and how the artist used them.

There are persistent symbols which have been handed down in time, although their meanings shift with use and period. The phoenix is such a symbol. We know it today as a strange allegorical bird which erects its own funeral pyre, is burned to death and then is gloriously resurrected. While the bird has always been associated with fire and resurrection, the uses to which this symbol has been put have changed through the ages. The legend of the bird has its dim origins in Eastern mythology variously associated with India, Assyria and Egypt. Some commentators believe that the word *Chol* in the book of *Job* applies to the phoenix. Classical writers such as Tacitus, Herodotus and Pliny record its rumored existence as a fact. By the Middle Ages the story of the phoenix came to be understood as a legend and therefore subject to the symbolical devices to which legends are put, and it was so used. In an early English poem an unknown translator took a classical poem called "The Phoenix" and altered it to mean the resurrection of Christ and all Christian souls burned in the fire of doomsday. Today we can see and hear the legend of the phoenix as used by Stravinsky for his own devices in the fairytale ballet *The Firebird*. In the Far East, in China, the phoenix had come to mean immortality. As such it was very often used as a stern decoration on the Foochow junks, surrounded by dragons symbolizing the immortal symbols of power, richness, greatness, independence, etc.

Perhaps true to a national reputation for being more interested in love than his neighbor across the Channel, a French poet (even then) was writing of love while the Englishman was resurrecting crisp Christians. In an early French poem called *The Romance of the Rose* some interpreters can see the direct use of sexual symbols in the employment of a phallic symbol in the use of a tower and another such implication in the vaginal flower, the rose.

In recent times our poets have become more obscure and less delicate in their use of symbols. In the work of many of these, the source of symbolical material comes from memory, persisting quotations or from obscure religious rituals and the symbols of an impoverished sexuality. These all can be found in Eliot's *The Waste Land*. Not the least of the modern thinking man's burden is the nagging question which rankles in his mind: "What does 'Datta Dayadhvam Damyata' really mean?" to say nothing of the queasy image of Kafka's cockroach which haunts him even when wide-awake.

Despite Eliot's three *D*'s and Kafka's man-insect, there are surprisingly consistent reactions to certain symbols, especially in graphics, depending upon the experience and psyche of the perceiver. This is, of course, the basis for the Rorschach tests. Colors have associative meanings for people. Red is the color not only of Communism, but of fire, war, turmoil; blue is the color of the sky, the peaceful sea, of hope. We thrill with horror at the red masque of death; the bluebird of happiness is a symbol of exactly what the name implies. To have such a common reaction of course requires the same basic background. In different societies where this is not the case, the same color may have opposing meanings. In our Western society the color for mourning is black; in China the mourners wear white.

One can create more subdivisions for the elements of communication with finer breakdowns of meaning. In painting the three means of classification—naturalism, formalism and symbolism—are perhaps the most inclusive. Painting has progressively used all three methods, but during the last half-century the mainstream of artistic creativity has been concentrated in symbolism. The modern artist, oppressed on the one hand by the weight and wealth of the magnificent past, the countless masterpieces which stand like so many unsurmountable peaks, and the unnerving representational precision of photography, gradually retreated to symbolism as an unchallengeable area of expression. In giving free rein to his individual expression he developed an intensely personal iconography which no longer contains communicable symbols.

Communication is the great bridge which links the artist and his public. It is the method by which people can understand the intention of the artist. Through its proper use, emotions can be evoked which extend beyond the simple meanings which lie in the commonplace depiction of things. Denied it, the perceiver is left without a clue to the artist's intention and must rely on his own subjective reactions, not always the same as the artist's, or he comes to rely on art Baedekers supplied by the *cognoscenti*. These he must accept at their face value without the inner conviction which grows from understanding.

Today the communicative power of painting has almost disappeared. It has come about through a series of changes which seem abrupt when compressed into a written history but which took place over a long period as artists reacted to changing motivations. At first, pictorial representation gave way to the sensation of the object itself as seen in impressionism, then post-impressionism, and in fauvism. It later grew into the idea of the object as in cubism and finally has changed into the artist's inner searching of his own responses. There is every evidence at hand to assume that this trend will continue and that we are nowhere near a return to an improved relationship between the artist and public, but that we are on the threshold of a period of anti-art. Contemporary art has communicated to one man at least, and the following is an excerpt from a column by the *Herald Tribune*'s roving commentator in Paris, John Crosby:

Me, I like art criticism to be brief and to the point, and it rarely is. Except when the artists start talking about each other. Then it's concise and deadly. The best short essay on contemporary art—it says everything, really— goes like this:

Mark Rothko, who painted pictures like this, drew the shade.

And Barney Newman, who painted pictures like this, shut the door.

And Ad Reinhardt, who painted pictures like this, turned out the lights.

Communication in Painting

The motivation for a painting has gone a long way since Leonardo da Vinci's doctrine, "A good painter is to paint two main things—namely, man and the working of man's mind." In the last hundred years the art of painting has been exploding like a string of fire-crackers. The kind of emotion and thought to be communicated through painting has shifted with kaleidoscopic suddenness. Once it was freed from its function as a mirror of the natural world, or even an esthetic comment about it, painting enjoyed a yeasty period of exploration in theory, form and invention.

In this revolutionary atmosphere two important

movements arose, one in France, the other in Germany. While they both broke incisively with the past, they took quite separate directions. They both were inheritors of the revolutionary tradition which had been passed along by the impressionists. The difference between the two, while slight at the moment of divergence, resulted in a vast gulf of separation as they mutually developed. Tragically, the German direction was halted by the First World War. The French direction maintained its vitality and for the next fifty years supplied most of the motivation and energy in the development of painting.

Essentially the difference lay in the fact that the French concerned themselves with esthetic problems and explored countless technical avenues of new uses of form and color. The Germans and Middle Europeans, on the other hand, sought to use the new liberation of means given them by the impressionists as a way to give greater artistic expression to their concern for human problems. Thus an immense difference was established, but its impact was barely grasped at the outset because intoxication with the new liberties was the headiest experience of the moment.

In France, the post-impressionists, Cézanne, Seurat, Matisse, Van Gogh, among many others, explored a multiplicity of new methods and theories. There was no cohesive school. The artists were rampantly individual. While each gave some new direction and power to the art of painting, he also was affected by the development going on around him.

Cézanne, a great innovator, took the freedom of color, the great gift of the impressionists, and fused it into a new concept of form. He was the strange anomaly of original creator and conservative and built his system on the classical compositional theories of Poussin and Lorrain, but succeeded in bringing a wholly new concept of plastic form into being which not only attained glorious heights of its own, but opened myriad doors to further development.

Seurat, with pointillism, influenced by new physical theories of light which were current, developed a new concept of color. He created the effect of a single color by the employment of groups of colors as components within a given area, an extension of the methods already being used by the impressionists. In his case, however, influenced by scientific investigations which were being made in the study of the phenomenon of light, the spectrum became very large, using a great range of opposites almost as in light itself. In addition, he sought to combine these new theories of light and color with the classical concepts of Renaissance composition.

Matisse explored the organization of form in space by reliance on color—mass and line—rather than by perspective, chiaroscuro and modeling. Van Gogh, a Dutchman by birth, a Middle European by inclination and a Frenchman in painting practice, instilled human passion into the everyday scene and object through using the new freedoms of color and form.

Through these revolutionary developments in the painters' means, the French artists gave a new vitality and force to their art. They actually intensified its communicative power, despite the fact that they had rejected traditional representation as it existed until then. However, they established the basis for involvement with esthetic problems alone, a tradition which persists today.

In Germany the new spirit, infused with the artistic ferment from France, manifested itself in a group of artists who called themselves the Blue Rider (*Der Blaue Reiter*), after a small painting by Wassily Kandinsky, one of its leaders. At about the same time evolved a movement known as *Die Brücke* (the Bridge), which influenced most of the important pre-World War I German and Scandinavian painters. Combined with their search for a new form of expression was the central concern for identity with human experience. They denounced man's reliance on a technological civilization as spiritually lazy and self-indulgent.

About 1910 German modern painting began to be called expressionism. It grappled with human rather than esthetic problems, although its artists sought to achieve their goals through esthetic means. Its goals were concisely defined by the Norwegian Edvard Munch, who wrote: "I want to show men who breathe, feel, love and suffer." Munch observed his credo with embarrassing candor. There exists a portrait of his friend the writer Przybyszewski, entitled "Jealousy." The writer, painted in bilious green, glares out of the foreground. Behind him his wife, quite naked, painted in red, stands beside her lover clad in black. We now know that Munch and the playwright Strindberg both vied for the favor of Przybyszewski's wife and Strindberg won out. It is Munch's jealousy which is staring out through the husband's eyes.

While this torment in paint was going on, the French artists concentrated more and more on technical problems. Though they acknowledged the importance of human emotions in art, they placed their prime stress on their individual esthetic emotions. Eventually they concluded that esthetics should not be involved with emotion at all, but motivated and disciplined by pure intellectuality. At this point art proliferated into cubism and from this into other theoretical deviations such as orphism, futurism and purism, all of them intellectual explorations.

Cubism, the most radical break with the past, had its roots in Cézanne's last explorations into the geometry of nature. There was no single kind of cubism, but there was one paramount rule underlying all kinds: a picture was to be constructed with known elements of reality, though without sensual or psychological expression. Communication, if any, was to be achieved solely by the play of plane, color and line.

The founders of cubism, Pablo Picasso and Georges Braque, while using somewhat similar means, brought to their art quite dissimilar personalities and purposes. Picasso, a prolific genius, used cubism as a way station on his road to other discoveries. His whole vibrant personality and work were governed by the avowed purpose to destroy what had gone before and start afresh. He thrust questions aside by his own affirmations. "I do not seek, I find," said he. When asked to explain his painting, he replied, "Do you ask a bird to explain his song?"

Braque was a more lyrical and sensitive artist, seeking to build from the past. Underlying his beautifully sensitive color was a rigidly intellectual motivation. His credo was, "I like the rule, the discipline which controls and corrects emotion." Again, defining his motivation, he said, "The subject is not the object of painting, but a new unity, the lyricism that results from method."

In terms of communication, cubism consisted of dimly recognizable subject matter arranged in planes. Its primary purpose was a technical one, to create depth while preserving a two-dimensional plane; to supplant perspective and modeling, the usual means of indicating depth, by the interposition of planes and the use of receding color, obeying a self-imposed restriction which was later set down by Jean Cocteau (Apollinaire's successor as impressario and communicator of art), "A picture is not a window."

With such a leap forward of freedom as cubism, all recognition of the object was abandoned. The schools tumbled into being. No holds were barred. The depiction of movement became the objective of the Italian futurists, with multiple visions of the same body in movement, a sort of superimposed stop-motion photography. In Switzerland and New York artists in revulsion from the First World War created a movement called Dada, an expression of disillusionment and anti-art. In Holland, *De Stijl* (the style) came into being. This last was the most coldly intellectual of them all. Piet Mondrian, one of its leading exponents, reduced form to areas delimited by right angles of verticals and horizontals, resulting in squares and rectangles. His color was reduced to primaries of white, black, red, yellow, blue. Mondrian's art has left an indelible imprint on modern architecture.

But as is normal in the ebb and flow of creativity, wherein each generation seeks its own place, the artists grew restless under the restraints imposed by so much cold intellectuality. Their need for self-expression drove them to seek something more personal, and within their own psyche they discovered a new well-spring of vitality. Painting became the product of liberated personality. Its source was the artist's inner being.

Now the floodgates stood wide open, and there poured forth a torrent of personal expression, much of it originating at a psychological level. Significant in this kind of painting is the work of the surrealists, Salvador Dali, Yves Tanguy and Max Ernst. With impeccable technique they portray a vision of a sub-conscious world which impresses some people by its power, but leaves the bulk of mankind wondering if it is art or nightmare. Painting has diverged from this direct exploration of the artist's neuroses, but to a great degree it is still motivated by the artist's inner urges toward self-identity rather than by the broader problems of humanity.

Communication, then, is no longer the primary interest of the modern artist. What he strives for is to induce a subjective response in the onlooker. Yet this loss of communication does not arise primarily from the technical complexities of the new esthetic. In the relatively rare instances when the modern artist desires to communicate, a strange esthetic imposes no un-scalable barrier to understanding and feeling. Rather, by identification with human emotion, he effects a heightened response. A masterly example is the large oil painting by Picasso titled "Guernica." Painted in 1937 for the Spanish Loyalist government as an exhibit in its pavilion at the Paris World's Fair, it combines contemporary esthetics with political comment. Picasso was emotionally committed to the Loyalist cause. The painting is his reaction to the bombing of the small town of Guernica by German planes flying for Franco. Yet the painting is in no sense reportorial.

The multiplicity of stations for the eye in its perspective, or rather lack of perspective, eliminates the sensation of reality. The distortion of familiar objects and the unexpected use of symbols such as a light bulb and a bull do not facilitate communication. But it is this very distortion, in the dying horse, the screaming mother, the dead child, that heightens the sense of agony, the horror of sudden death from the sky. In the extreme delineation of muscular and emotional tension, conveyed by deliberate dehumanization of the mother, we can almost hear her screams.

To many this picture communicates more emotion about Guernica than all the words and photographs ever published, such is the artist's great compassion and dreadful anger. To be sure, the picture does not communicate emotion to everybody in the same degree, but it powerfully affects a large number of people. The fact that many can be made to feel a directed emotion, in this case a response to social injustice, through an esthetic statement indicates that artists and laymen can again be brought together in common humanity within a framework of esthetics.

Another modern painter able to communicate

within this framework was the late Paul Klee. In a mood quite apart from the thunder of Picasso, gentle, poetic, almost childlike, he infused his canvases with a sense of magic and wonder. In his "Twittering Machine" he depicted a preposterous contraption consisting of spidery lines in a seemingly logical mechanical order. From one side projects a crank, a birdlike device perches on the top, and we know at once that when the crank turns, the whole foolish machine will come joyously to life and the bird will twitter away. Indeed, the spidery delicacy of the drawing seems to be atwitter already.

These are two examples which, though diverse in style and subject, both evoke a universal human response.

The geographical center of art now has moved to the United States. It is a restless art. In a few short years two vastly different schools have come into prominence. Today it is pop art. Just yesterday it was action painting which had its source in the work of Kandinsky, who gave birth to many schools of painting in his passage through the world of art. Kandinsky, who found himself as an expressionist, later suppressed all reality to abstract arrangement of form and color. His force as an articulator of new theories was felt by nearly everyone with whom he came in contact. An unusual result was the transfer of his color theories to music. They can be heard in the works of Scriabine, particularly his color tone poems *Prometheus* and *Poem of Ecstasy,* which were written at a time when Scriabine was strongly influenced by Kandinsky. In his painting he compressed into his canvases the intellectually abstract form and the passion of color. His work was controlled and deliberate. He opened a veritable Pandora's box of art.

His spiritual inheritors, the American school of abstract expressionists, again reacting against the restraint of so much intellectuality, resorted to a method which closely approximated automatism. The leaders of the school, Hans Hoffman, Jackson Pollock, Willem de Kooning, Franz Kline, described their painting as an act of self-discovery. Though recognition is totally absent, considerable visual impact is achieved through bold form, strong color contrast and a rugose, tactile quality. Strong and violent, the effect offers limitless scope for subjective response.

At least two of the painters, Pollock and Kline, developed highly personal, easily identifiable styles. Pollock constructed his paintings from a semi-controlled fall of paint, dripping and throwing it on the canvas wth a physical vigor quite evident in the final result.

Kline created an impenetrable ideography by slashing at huge white canvases with crude black strokes. This simplified organization in these big areas produces a feeling of great strength. The size of the canvas is in itself important, because the simple idea gains power by enlargement. The effect is inescapable. The sheer violence compels subconscious response. But it communicates nothing whatever of humanity. Undeniably original, forceful and spontaneous to the point of improvisation, it remains incomprehensible to all but a small audience. It is a private art. Moreover, it is no sooner stated than it has been stated once for all. To keep repeating it, as the abstract expressionists do, must be an act of considerable will, since each time they must re-energize the spontaneity.

In his book *Conversations with Artists,* Selden Rodman quotes Adolph Gottlieb, an abstract expressionist, as follows: ". . . The abstract expressionist says to the public, 'You're stupid. We despise you. We don't want you to like us or our art.' " And again, "I'd like more status than I have now, but not at the cost of closing the gap between artist and public. I'd like to widen it!" It is probably unfair to tar all abstract expressionists with Mr. Gottlieb's brush. Nevertheless, his remarks reflect the withdrawal of many a contemporary artist.

The spell and fashion of the abstract expressionists seem presently to have run their course. Prophesying in art is as useless as prophesying history. But in all probability, those whose reputations were made during its popularity will continue to find a public. Abstract expressionism will leave an indelible imprint on the course of painting and become another historic backwater in art like cubism and surrealism, as art seeks to rejoin its own mainstream. Already questions are being asked which but a short time ago would not have been voiced. Indicative is the question of the art critic Emily Genauer, who writes: "The mystery of Rothko's paintings is only equaled by the mystery of the source of his reputation."

It was inevitable that an art so devoid of human contact, once having run its course of shock and amazement, would peter out. Its new resources can come only from greater shock and increased technical sleight of hand. This has never been a sound foundation for any art.

Now, again, we see reaction set in in the new painter looking for an individual self-expression, opening another windowless room in the house of art. A neo-Dadist movement of anti-art is emerging called pop art. It is very diverse and no consistent image has yet appeared. It has just received an enormous boost in status. The Biennale in Venice has awarded first prize to Rauschenberg, the American pop artist. The art shares in common large-scale, crude renditions of everyday objects, from enlargements of the funnies to a painting of a flag to a hamburger sandwich. Collage, too, has returned. In keeping with our times it is giant size—whole bed springs, trousers, chairs, are affixed to the painted panel. It seems a last convulsion of disgust with art. The only thing encouraging about its presumed short stay on the art scene, short at least in terms of the history of art, is that the artists are groping again for some human content, and for the moment seem so ashamed of themselves that they sneer at the very act. It is at least a hopeful sign, even in anti-art. In all probability public awareness of the art will be extremely rapid. This is due to an electronic phenomenon of our time, television. Abstract expressionism was very difficult to telecast. The formlessness of the content and dependence upon scale, texture and color made it a hard subject for telecasting. Now the TV people have something they can use. In addition, the content lends itself to endless comment and witticisms.

Nevertheless as long as the artist strives for communication, however strange the language or symbol, he has the right to demand that we understand him.

For art is a language, expressing feelings impossible to express in any other way, and language is a communication by mutually understood symbols. While one may respond to a painting without being able to explain the response, if these symbols become too remote, the language places an excessive burden on the auditor and may lead him to a subjective re-creation distinct from the original intent, or the public may abandon any hope of spirituality or profundity in art and accept it at its face value, as decoration, as space fillers, to fit the varying purposes of the artifacts of living. It will be used and abandoned as is fashion. On the other hand, the power of some of these new esthetics to evoke a subjective response, however indefinable, cannot be dismissed. They hold the promise that if artists re-establish communication, they will have the means to do so with an energy and directness never before possible.

This is the present state of communication in painting. For the moment the prevailing *isms* seem to record a private anguish—the travail of artists trying to rid themselves of everything they know in the attempt to find a new beginning. But painting is a most potent and persuasive art. Its effect on other arts is enormous. Because of its vigor and early liberation, it, more than any other art, helped to establish the climate for the dehumanization prevalent in all of the arts. Because of the esthetic forces now unloosed, the other arts may no longer be as responsive to direct influence. But a return to a concern for the communication of human experience in painting undoubtedly will stimulate such concern in all the arts.

Communication in Sculpture

Sculpture, too, is an art which is developing in directions divorced from the commonalty of man. In tune with an esthetic which shows little responsibility either to itself or to the needs of mankind, it is departing radically from its most recent past. It is unfair, perhaps, to identify the work of Epstein, Lipschitz, Moore or Marini with the past, yet despite the fact that some of these men still are alive and at work, in terms of current esthetic standards they are of the past. Under the goad of an unreasoning urgency toward radical change which motivates most creative work today, sculptors are turning their backs upon a period which has produced deeply moving, beautiful, often lyrical works, to launch into a wide-ranging exploration of incomprehensible forms.

The range in creative efforts goes from tortured lumps of metal as they partially break out of a mold, to stray pieces of metal shards in haphazard arrangement, to the exquisite and precise linearity of forms in space. Sculpture, once a most eloquent expression of human emotion, now offers the choice of sensuous delight usually filled by the enjoyment of chandeliers, architectural screens, or the mystical pleasure of poring over inchoate incunabula.

Sculpture has come to rely heavily upon sensate response for any communicability. It has not yet reached the level of obscurity that contemporary painting has achieved, since the image of man has not yet fallen into as deep disrepute in the motivation of sculpture as in painting. This perhaps is due to the fact that sculpture started its revolutionary process later than painting did and has not yet had time to complete its alienation by total submission to a dominant academy of the left. There are still a few giants such as Moore and Lipschitz who stem the tide running so strongly toward estrangement.

Sculpture was unprepared by its historical development for the impact of the new concept of art for art's sake and therefore turned to painting as its guide and mentor. At the beginning of this century, sculptors who were moved to explore the new art did so under the guidance of the painters' esthetics. For that matter, many of the painters of the period were sculptors as well—Daumier, Degas and Renoir, followed later by

Matisse, Picasso and Braque, and others. All of these extended their painter theories and ideas into sculpture.

Sculptors of this first period of change had great difficulty in loosening the ties with their past. The great ferment was in painting. Its theorists were persuasive, articulate and urgent. They made painting a dominant, infectious and influential art. No artist of any stamp or métier could avoid its influence. Yet it was difficult at the outset for the sculptors to synthesize ideas erupting around them into a form of their own, and therefore they resorted to imitation, so that during the transitory period of cubism in painting, cubist sculpture was in transit as well.

This imitative effort was in itself not an easy one to bring off successfully, since there was a significant barrier to ready adaption. Painting theory was involved with the preservation of the two-dimensional reality of the canvas, and sculpture is inescapably a three-dimensional entity. Its problem always had been solved within an esthetic framework concerned with form, mass and volume as its exists in space; and line, texture and color as it exists in light.

Beyond the physical difficulty inherent in transplanting an idea from one medium to another was the psychological block in ridding itself of its tradition. Sculpture was haunted and dominated by its past. It was magnificent with the Egyptians when painting was relatively primitive.

In the centuries since the giants of the Renaissance, only a few sculptors' names emerge. All but one of these, Rodin, are remembered not as great revolution-

ary originators, but as significant contributors to their
age, working with variations within the great tradition.
Those who stood out were Bernini in the 17th century,
Houdon in the 18th and Canova in the 19th. Rodin
in the latter half of the 19th century brought a new
passion and power to the art. But the step from Rodin
to modern sculpture was enormous. Modern sculpture
is therefore a 20th-century creation—suddenly, hardly
anticipated, a great leap forward. There is no long
revolutionary line of ancestors to indicate evolutionary
process. Unlike painting, it did not have seminal, gradually emerging, originating sources. There was no
Turner, Goya, Constable, Delacroix or Courbet. Sculpture's processes of change were compressed into a relatively short period of time.

Beyond the lack of revolutionary sources was the
nature of the art in relation to its public. Painting
makes fewer demands on its public; therefore, esthetics in painting has greater built-in motility. Its esthetics
can shift more rapidly because painting is a private
art. An audacious painter needs only a small coterie
or even a single patron to support him. Sculpture
through the centuries had become a public art. It was
either monumental or commemorative, or was used
as a landscape or architectural accessory.

All of these conservative elements affecting change
stood in the way of sculpture on the threshold of the
revolutionary 20th century. This makes the explosive
development of sculpture an even more extraordinary
event than that of painting. But the revolution once
begun, and under an influence as strong as modern
painting, sculpture has followed it into the same ex-

ploratory searching of means, and borrowed the same philosophical certainty that as an art it should be concerned only with its own esthetic experience. In the ensuing years, encouraged by a willing acceptance which still lends its ready support, and because of the persuasive influence of painting, certain sculptures have reached the same level of incomprehensibility and anti-art as have paintings.

However, the power of painting as motivation and model has its limits. Sculpture has one overruling physical characteristic. It exists as a volume in space and therefore has an utterly different capability in its power to communicate or to evoke. As an example, a Calder mobile shares many of the amorphous design devices that appear in a Joan Miró or Yves Tanguy painting, yet it engenders an entirely different set of responses in the observer. In the paintings, the devices appear on the flat canvas plane. In the Tanguy they are arranged in a deep linear perspective; in Miró the devices appear on the single surface in a two-dimensional composition. Any meaning or reaction that these paintings evoke is based on a subconscious associative response.

In the case of the mobile there is a direct physical response. The mobile hangs in space in a minutely adjusted balance. The parts move in a constantly shifting relationship, one to another. They provide pleasure in the manner in which they fill space, while giving no meaning whatsoever. The dimensional nature of the art therefore forces recognition of remembered forms, real or imaginary, and the actual physical experience of an object in space. All objects exist for us as three-dimensional volumes. In painting, the reality of space and volume is indicated rather than experienced. The indication is achieved by a range of methods, partially by direct visual experience and in part by intellectual indication. In the direct manner, the use of pictorial realism, perspective and chiaroscuro (modeling in light and shade) are employed. In the nonrealist or nonobjective art we must rely on devices such as the interposition of planes or lines, one upon another, or by the use of advancing or receding color to establish the idea of space and the volumes that fill it. For that reason, it becomes easier to lose the object entirely in painting. In a completely subjective painting no attempt is made to define space. The work exists as a two-dimensional ideograph not related to objects or space, or for that matter to any known experience. Therefore, the very fact that sculpture exists in dimensional volume gives it a direct physical relationship to human experience that provides an inborn evocative power. Because of this innate evocative power in sculpture, painting and sculpture cannot continue parallel, but will diverge, despite the sameness of the ruling esthetic. With the sudden displacement of abstract expressionism by pop art, painting gives indication of a radical shift in direction, while the future turnings of sculpture are less certain.

Since its revolutionary inception at the turn of the century, the two arts have followed the same developmental pattern. It is important to recognize this in order to provide the basis for an informed judgment, freed from the cant which accompanies each daring venture into a new kind of experiment.

The sculptor who only partially influenced the future direction, but who was a catalyst in preparation for the 20th-century development of the art, was Auguste Rodin, who lived and worked in the latter half of the 19th century. As in the case of the painters of his period, his work was motivated by a strong reaction to the existing academies. Sculpture had become ultra-formalistic, polished and idealized. Rodin rejected that which was around him and returned to nature with power and passion. It is a foible of our time to comb the work of past giants for aspects which give assurances and respectable antecedents to tendencies and beliefs operative today. By doing this, in one fell stroke it is possible to identify present work with the mainstream of art and to brush off any questions as to whether the present work has validity and is truly a basic development instead of an exotic backwash.

Rodin's work is subjected to that sort of scrutiny. It speaks magnificently for his art that in his work the experts can find whatever they wish. It can provide nearly everyone with reassurance and direction. But however individual cultists present various aspects of his work, the fact remains that he was a very great master, immersed in every level of creativity, the most pre-eminent of which were his content, his ideas, always conceived in human terms. Man was Rodin's subject. He said, "The human body is a temple that marches. It is a moving architecture." He was an instinctive expressionist before the term was identified as a school of art. Without losing much in naturalistic delineation, he ran the gamut of invention and exploration of his medium. He worked with single architectural masses existing in space, he worked with partial forms emerging from the unfinished block, and he worked with groupings of separated figures, individually existing in space, yet with finite relationship one to another.

After the fresh wind of Rodin blew through the sculptors' ateliers, there was a split of the art into tangential directions. Some took the Michelangelo-Rodin concept of form emerging from the block, creating a version of impressionism in which the major elements of an ideated form were expressed with all lesser detail suppressed.

Such an artist was Medardo Rosso, who began as a painter and who in a sense retained the qualities of an impressionist painter. Like a Monet painting in which the image emerges from the canvas by almost imperceptible means, so Rosso's sculpture emerges from the block. His usual medium, wax, lent itself to these ephemeral transitions. His subjects were the very antithesis of the heroic. Genre scenes were his favorite subject, indicated rather than spelled out.

Bourdelle, on the other hand, was influenced by the passionate qualities of Rodin, and his work always was achieved with expressionist power. He was, however, influenced by the eclectic searchings current in the École des Beaux Arts at the time. His subject matter and treatment show an attempt to recapture for sculpture the simplicity and strength of the older forms by a return to the archaic and fifth-century Greek sculpture. He was saved from a dry eclecticism by his power and vitality. At an opposite pole was the work of

Maillol. Instead of dwelling upon the power and passion inherent in a subject, his was a return to a serene naturalism, but shorn of all the slick convention of the academy. Nearly everything he had to say was said in terms of the nude female figure, but without the nubile or erotic inferences. His work expressed a homely virtue rather than heroic beauty. He was able to achieve an extraordinary combination of architectonic mass, at the same time retaining the feeling of life and of the eternal female.

These were the prevailing tendencies in France and they were followed to a large degree in Germany, although in that country the emphasis given to human experience by painting had its influence on sculpture. Such an underlying motivation can be seen in the work of the sculptors Lehmbruck, Barlach, Kollwitz.

Lehmbruck's works are filled with an inner sadness. As his art developed, it tended to become elongated and increasingly expressive. The elongation heightened the communication of spiritual melancholy without appearing to create an unnatural distortion. Barlach found his sources in folk art. His work reflects the qualities of immediacy inherent in medieval and folk art, its subject matter concerned with the human emotions of joy, anger and pain told in simplified expressionist forms. Kollwitz brought to sculpture the sensitivity of a graphic artist. Her work contains a deep feeling of identity with human grief and suffering told in terms of her human compassion and her artistic terms of compact sculptural mass with detail suppressed.

Up until this point sculpture was involved with

humanistic representation. The first great break came in Paris with the Rumanian sculptor Constantin Brancusi. That he was first apprenticed to a carpenter, undoubtedly developed his understanding and respect for essential structure in form. However, his artistic urges led him to Paris and the study of sculpture. Despite the great reputation of Rodin, Brancusi showed his independence of character by turning down an invitation to work in that master's studio. His friendship with the painter Modigliani put him into the center of the swirling esthetic revolution. Brancusi, while never quite departing entirely from ideated form, became the first significant abstractionist. He reduced ideas and objects to a form either recognizable or at least identifiable. His famous "Bird in Flight" was an expression of upward soaring. His pipe-like torsos or egg-shaped heads all were geometrical essences of natural forms.

Brancusi, though disavowing Rodin, was the important link between the liberator Rodin and the free-ranging sculpture of today. Fundamentally he sought to reduce known forms to essential statements while rejecting any allegorical, historical or literary allusion. He held the nature of his material and the subject matter in equilibrium. He looked not only for the essence of his subject matter, but for the essence of his material. Marble and bronze were polished; stone and wood, roughhewn.

In the work of Brancusi and Archipenko, who followed, we see the first major shift from content to means. Although both of these artists used recognizable objects as a basis for their content, Archipenko, a Russian transplant to Paris, was influenced by the cubist experiments going on around him and exhibited with them. He later added the painter's device of collage to his basic medium. While this opened the door for exploration by others, it had the effect of turning his own work into a mannered and decorative art.

Zadkine was another sculptor much influenced by cubism, from which he never wandered very far except for isolated forays into expressionism. But it was Jacques Lipschitz who used cubism for a springboard into a powerful expressionist art. Lipschitz, too, indicated his intense desire to discard all vestiges of the past. Once told that Rodin admired one of his works, his rejoinder was, "What's so wrong with my little piece of sculpture?"

Cubism was the great catalyst for sculpture. It opened the way for all manner of exploration and enabled sculptors to isolate the essential problems of sculpture unhampered by likeness or representation. An additional impetus was given by the painter-sculptors Modigliani, Picasso, Matisse, Braque, Derain, Léger and many others who made adaptations of their painter art, bringing a fresh, nonsculptural point of view to the art of sculpture. Liberated from representation, sculpture also abandoned the time-honored concept that it was essentially a volume that existed in space. This concept was amended to contain the idea that a volume can be penetrated or hollow. It held that just as a mass or volume existed in space, so space could exist within volume. Space could move through the volume in the same manner as the volume moves in space.

Inevitably this led to the belief that the direction of space should be defined, and so constructivist sculptures came into being. Fundamentally these were abstract geometric arrangements or constructions in which planes and lines of the sculpture defined the voids which they surrounded. The two leading constructivists were the Russians Naum Gabo and his brother, Antoine Pevsner. Gabo had met that very persuasive theorist Kandinsky in 1910, and by 1920 he and his brother were ready to publish their artistic credo. They had been teaching in Moscow along with Kandinsky, Tatlin and Malevitch, all abstractionists, when they wrote their Realist Manifesto. It renounced volume and mass in favor of planes and lines as the basic perception of their time. This was the start of a most powerful influence which pervades sculpture to this day and was the authoritarian cleavage away from human experiential motivations.

The idea of representation was, however, still too strong to be entirely abandoned, but now, influenced by the newer ideas, the artists who were still motivated by the human form joined in the production of a powerfully moving sculptural art. While still deriving from natural form in that human and animal figures were recognizable, they employed the concepts of hollow and penetrated form and the simplification and drama of expressionism. The artists of this period and direction, while intensely personal, all have the same communicative power. They all make a statement about man, poetic, dramatic or lyrical, as the case may be. Epstein, Moore and Marini cover such a span of emotion. Even now, at a time when sculpture develops a new sensation every week, the simple, dramatic depiction of the Virgin and Child by Epstein, which adorns the convent wall in London's Cavendish Square, overwhelms one with its majestic power. The serene beauty of a Henry Moore family group in an open park gives a feeling of continuity of man. Despite the first strangeness of the sculpture in its distortion of forms leading away from reality, the spirit of the love of mankind still shines through. Marini's sensual, lyrical horses and riders are in a great, perhaps Oriental, tradition of beauty of art in spite of his subtle mutation of naturalistic forms. Less realistic but equally moving is Lipschitz in his "Song of the Vowels," an expressionist work in a harplike form, singing of man's intoxication and joy over his power of speech. This is a random sampling of the beauty and power which the new freedoms brought to sculpture.

However, with the restlessness prevalent in all of the arts, the onrushing art of sculpture hardly hesitated long enough to savor the qualities that had emerged, much less to examine and expand these directions, but plunged headlong into new personal expressions. The English expressionists Reg Butler, Kenneth Armitage and Lynn Chadwick have made their own personal dramatic contributions, but the humanistic tradition, while not entirely lost, is suppressed. Sculpture is the most significant and vital art expression to come out of England in this century, and, in keeping with the poetic English tradition of humanism, the sculptures have not entirely lost their identity with this national tradition. The work of this group, however, clearly indicates the borderland between the bounds of the human tradition and the inchoate unknown beyond.

Sculpture has arrived at a complete break with the human tradition. Up until this point the departure had been made by the constructivists alone. Now most of the younger sculptors are concentrated in this direction. As in the case of painting, the equilibrium between idea and means has been broken with means in the ascendancy; and, as in the case of painting, the exploration spreads out in all directions.

Abstract expressionism is represented in the work of Roszak and Lipton, powerful, dark and impenetrable. The forms grow out of their materials and techniques. The controlled and accidental use of metal in casting, brazing, forging and welding has created a sculpture which at once contains the element of planned construction and improvised expressionism. The subjects are darkly romantic, holding onto meaning only through their titles and the vaguely suggestive actuality of the form in space. David Smith works with welded and inscribed steel in sculpture which stands somewhere between geometric shape and freer organic form. Constructivism continues to hold a fascination for a group of sculptors who find within the limiting boundaries of the approach opportunities to be dramatic, playful or decorative.

In its newest turnings, sculpture has at last turned to anti-art and seeming disgust with our society. This is seen in the "found object," "junk" sculpture or improvisation. Out of the detritus of a mechanical society with its junk yards, automobile graveyards and other repositories of the moldering remains of once precise and functioning machines and implements, artists are erecting assemblies in the name of sculpture. The art has burst through any borders of containment and seemingly anything goes and anything is valid. As in the case of other arts, we are now in a period of unrestrained originality.

And so sculpture continues its development, somewhat parallel to painting, and slowly but inevitably reaching a point of complete estrangement and the condition of being an instrument of alienation added to those which already burden man's existence. Already the despair and disbelief in any deeper motivation than the endless fascination with means is taking its toll of the relationship of man and one of his treasured arts. To the neo-Dada and anti-art represented by such things as massive blocks of crushed automobile parts and assemblies of junk, self-destroying sculpture has been recently added. It is planned and timed to amaze and make the evening deadline of the newspapers. These creations are being sponsored by responsible dealers and museums.

In one aspect of the constructivist school the work tends increasingly toward a decorative space-filling character, and if history repeats itself this kind of art will reap the reward that strictly decorative, mannered art always has earned, an honored oblivion. Curiously, when the subject and technique are in accord, such as in Lippold's "Sun," which is in the Metropolitan Museum, the creation is an evocative work of great beauty. But when the same technique is used as a space delineator over the bar of a restaurant in the Seagram building, it has all the shimmer and glisten of a chandelier, but loses its meaning as sculpture.

Contemporary architects respond to this kind of sculpture, since both the newer architecture and this form of sculpture have their motivational sources in the same precise structural linearity. Therefore, this kind of sculpture is much used in contemporary architecture. There is another Lippold in the lounge area of the Philharmonic Hall in New York. The lounges of this hall always create in me a compulsive expectation that I am about to hear an announcement of TWA Flight #600 X leaving for Erewhon. The sculpture is called "Orpheus and Apollo," although some irreverent souls have named it the Exploding Woodpile. It does not successfully utilize the space, since it is difficult to see it or experience it from any vantage point within the building. It appears at its best from outside the building, where isolated parts create an interesting pattern when seen through the blank staring windows. The principal evocative power of this sculpture is as a decorative space filler.

In the same lounge, to one side, is Bourdelle's expressionist mask of Beethoven, which evokes the spirit of that tortured creator whose great voice still roars across the years and fills the hall, that imperfect hi-fi instrument, with the sound of genius.

And so, in a few impatient years, we have come to the present dilemma in sculpture. Is its continuance to be lodged in further excesses of technical exploration, or will its future development be in the direction of a return to the humanistic disciplines? Herbert Read, in an essay on *De Stijl,* voices the opinion that it is doubtful whether our humanistic civilization can dispense with the figurative symbol without profound changes in its spiritual condition.

But even with such philosophical consideration set aside, there remains the pragmatic question as to whether an art based solely on technical disciplines and theories, not refreshed with the vital sources of life itself, will not generate into an academy emptier and more arid than those which grew from realism. In addition, there is the lateral effect of a dehumanized sculpture on another art, such as architecture, and its collateral effect, along with the other dehumanized arts, on our society.

Communication Through Form and Symbol: World's Fairs

Nearly everyone has pleasurable memories of a fair. It is a festival of fun, excitement and of the cock-eyed world of the future. Under all of this visible pleasure-making and educational surface are purposes of utmost seriousness. It is here that individuals, corporations and nations try to win sympathy and approval from large audiences by presenting themselves in the most favorable light possible.

It all takes place under highly competitive circumstances with each entity on display in direct competition with another which has the same purposes in mind, an attempt to capture the same loyalties.

To accomplish these ends every available device of communication is used.

Since fairs have become international in scope and the barriers of language difference must be overcome, there is a heavy reliance on form and symbolism as vehicles of communication. Fairs still are a market place disguised as a carnival. They also are the distillation of communication problems and principles.

Fairs have their early roots in harvest-market traditions. They were a necessity in an agricultural society. Because of the dispersal of a thinly settled populace, the limited means of travel and the lack of a wide-reaching communication method, fairs grew up as a device by which numbers of people with common interests could be brought together at a stated time and for a stated purpose—for the exchange of goods and ideas.

Whether the idea of the fun was a natural concomitant of large numbers of people gathered after a period of hard work, or whether the presence of so large an audience brought in the jongleurs, acrobats, masters of dancing bears, is immaterial. The fact is that the tradition of entertainment persists to this day. For that matter, now, when communication methods can bring news of discoveries and products instantaneously to people, a purpose once filled by fairs, entertainment, either by direct means or through educational methods, has become the backbone of fair techniques.

World's fairs are the inheritors of this long tradition. Some of the things within the tradition still go on, others have changed drastically or else have altogether disappeared. In the middle of the 19th century, with the expansion of the industrial revolution, fairs became a display place for structural concepts. A world's fair still is an architectural showcase where architecture is permitted to be experimental and fanciful. Many of the significant breakthroughs in design and structural application first happened at fairs.

A fair still is a place at which to assemble the wonders of the world whenever possible. Remote societies and cultures are introduced to the public at large and many important influences on the arts can be dated from a time at which they were first seen or heard at a fair. This is true of Oriental music and dance and of African sculpture.

Other things have changed radically. The fair no longer is a useful device for the small producer. Once it was the only means by which a small producer could gain recognition and approval. The cake-baking or pickle-tasting competitions were a microcosm of that function.

Even for the larger producer, some of the purposes of a fair no longer are useful. Once beer and ketchup bottle labels swarmed with reproductions of world's fair medals. They announced that the product had won world-wide acclaim from a group of Apollonian judges at a fair. It gave a stamp of world-wide approval to their product and became a basis for selling claims. TV and magazine advertising have replaced the world's fair as a device to make these claims. Now they simply reiterate the claim of a product's excellence and achieve their purposes with a larger audience and without the need of direct competition on any but their own terms.

Larger corporations have come to use fairs as a giant public relations platform. While they do not engage in direct sales, every means short of this is used to attract favorable attention to the company and its products. In the last several decades a new group of exhibitors has come to the fore—the national pavilions of interested countries. These are erected in order to garner sympathy and approval, to help in fostering trade, tourism or acceptance of ideology. It is in this latter group, the national pavilions, that we can see the arts of communication and the communication of arts most intellectually, powerfully or subtly used.

Symbols

With the growing intensity of the ideological challenge, leading powers have found a fair to be a valuable instrument by which to explain themselves and place themselves in the most favorable propaganda light. The fair exhibit has become an invaluable platform from which to advance a national posture and image.

Millions of people are attracted, but the nature and temper of their attendance places certain strictures on the kind of communication symbols which can be used for greatest effectiveness. People come to a fair to be entertained and stimulated. But soon they encounter the factor of fatigue, physical fatigue from walking countless miles and mental fatigue from the overwhelming wealth of information, sights and impressions to be registered and comprehended in a compressed period of time. In addition, comparison plays an important role because the movement from one exhibit to another is rapid. Immediacy and impact are mandatory. So many impressions cry for consideration that the visitor subconsciously picks and chooses, giving his attention only to the things which capture his imagination or, conversely, which activate some familiar chord of response or associative experience.

The communication task in a fair exhibit generally is organized in the following way: the first need is to establish an over-all theme which sets the mood and direction for the total complex. After the theme and its interpretation are set, then a "main tent" attraction is developed. This is a central attention getter which rivets interest and stages the platform from which individual exhibits are later developed with more detailed information. The totality of exhibits and buildings is aimed at an over-all communication goal.

A great deal of sophistication in the methods of conveying a desired message has been developed over the years. This has come about by the increased skills available but even more so by the need to disguise the propaganda line or sales message. Since people come to a fair for entertainment, stimulation, education, any device which does not recognize this mood and temper would be rejected subconsciously. Therefore, direct propaganda statements are avoided, and exhibits use a wealth of form symbols to advance their cause by more subtle means.

The New York World's Fair of 1964 unfortunately has not won the right to be considered a world's fair by the international body which rules on such matters. It does not therefore have as many large national pavilions. The Brussels World's Fair of 1958 was the last such important occasion. It was the first great fair after the war, and all the major countries were seriously participating. It was an extraordinary and unsettled time in Europe. Most countries still were digging out of the painful holocaust. Former allies and enemies now were individually contending for the public heart and mind, trying to get the most sympathetic and favorable consideration. They were making an intense effort to prove to the millions in attendance that a given system was the most viable and promising. In short, every propaganda line was being used, but under the most sophisticated sort of masking.

The mood of the European people in the year 1958 was an admixture of hope and despair. Fear of atomic war, faltering economies, contributed to the anxiety. But since hope springs eternal in the human breast, there was an eager search for signs of reassurance. In words the mood was perhaps best expressed in a quotation by Martin Luther which was emblazoned in many languages on a huge panel which dominated the entrance in the German pavilion: EVEN IF I KNEW THAT TOMORROW THE WORLD WOULD COME TO AN END, I WOULD STILL PLANT MY APPLE TREE TODAY.

With this sort of prevailing mood it was interesting and instructive to see how each country responded to the communication challenge. Each country told its story according to its individual purpose. Viewed as communication, some were magnificent; others were failures.

The Netherlands pavilion was one which used symbolism most effectively in its architecture and displays. The central impression one carried away was that this was a people possessed of an indomitable fighting spirit who would win against all adversity. The organizing theme was their fight against the ravages of a relentless sea in its onslaughts on their low-lying land. The "main tent show" was a huge glass tank containing a sloping gravel bank at one end to approximate a cross section through a Dutch beach. It was filled with water, and a mechanical device caused waves to roll along the long length of the tank, finally to crash and break on the beach. Posts with electronic devices attached were embedded in the bank to measure the force of the waves and the degree of the ensuing erosion. Panel inscriptions announced this to be the method of vigilance set up on the Holland coast. The sheer movement of the water as it rolled the length of the tank was fascinating.

Secondary exhibits developed the manner in which this primary information was used for anti-erosion work and for giant land reclamation projects. Additional exhibits rounded out Holland's cultural life, all keyed to the central idea of Holland and the sea. Holland's involvement with the sea was used in its historical and art exhibits and in its display of trade functions. The message was clear: these were a historically brave, intelligent people fighting their way back into the sun against great adversity and against a giant elemental adversary, the sea.

The British pavilion was a remarkable solution, in some ways the most subtly successful propaganda device at the fair. What made it so extraordinary was that in these times of radical and libertarian ideas the British gave the greatest promise of continuity of existence through an oblique view of their monarchial institution. The device used was an exhibit of the symbols of monarchy through England's long and glorious history. The exhibit complex was entered through a small chapel-like building replete with dim lighting and modern stained glass effects. One was not able to roam at will, but rather was conducted in single file past the exhibits in a ceremonial manner. The very nature of the file past resulted in a hushed and worshipful attitude. As a matter of fact, one cynical and worldly friend said of it later, "It was amazing. I felt as though it would be sacrilegious to wear my hat and speak in anything above a whisper."

On the right hand were the symbols of pomp and circumstance, the crown, orbs, scepter and chalices used in the enthronement of English kings almost since the monarchy was founded. On the left side were mannequin figures wearing the historic robes and uniforms of attendants at these periods of history. On the darkened wall at the end of the room was a single object, the Annigoni portrait of the Queen glowing out of the dark wall through the hidden lights directed on it.

The visitor, on seeing this vast pageant of historic continuity through the relics of the enthronement of kings leading to the present monarch, was moved by the unspoken conviction that here was proof that man and his institutions would survive. These were the symbols of centuries-long continuance in the face of the travail of a nation and her kings.

On leaving the chapel-like structure one read a message which in effect said, "This is a record of our past glory and history. Through this door are our plans for the future." One then walked into the British Industries Fair. It was filled with exhibits of city planning, housing, technical developments, machinery and so on. It was a most successful exhibit, for through various symbols it gave demonstrations of England's durability and promise and thereby touched the deep longings and aspirations of the millions who saw it. The visitors identified themselves with its message and therefore the British message had the most sympathetic audience. It was a brilliantly conceived use of idea and symbol and employment of techniques.

Another exhibit more forthright in its message was the Israeli pavilion. The purpose of this exhibit was clearly stated by the nature of the material chosen and the way it was shown. The building was simple and straightforward. Upon entering, the visitor immediately was confronted with a geographical, historical and archeological display which in effect proclaimed that the Jews had several millennia of identification with the soil and land of Israel and therefore were entitled to it. While the message was forthright enough, it was softened by the nature of the archeological displays, not the least of which was a fragment of a recent archeological find, the Dead Sea scrolls, with translations in several languages.

From this first exhibit the visitor passed through a section which explained the reason that the Jews would not get out of Israel, no matter what threats or pressures were employed. The device here was the history of the oppressions they had suffered, but centered mainly on the six million Jews that had been killed by the Nazis. Having established this, the rest of the pavilion devoted itself to a demonstration of how the land was to be used—hopeful and positive. In all, it was a most successful propaganda message, clothed in architecture and exhibit devices.

Austria was another country which chose history as an exhibit device. In this case the major unit upon which they relied to create sympathy was the fact that Vienna had been the home of music's historical greats. Holograph copies were on display by Mozart, Haydn, Beethoven and Schubert on to Schönberg, Webern and Berg, all providing mute testimony to Vienna's great musical heritage. An adjunct to this display was a demonstration that this was not just history, but rather it was a tradition still going on. A studio was set up in which young men and women who were student members of various quartet and trio groups received instruction in ensemble playing from a teacher. This instruction took place in the presence of visitors. It had the impact of immediacy and participation. Art was used to establish a bond of sympathy with the visitors.

The Russian building achieved an important propaganda effect suited to its own needs. Russia, too,

had suffered the ravages of war, but instead of focus-
ing on success or continuity against adversity, the
main purpose of the exhibit was to demonstrate
achievement by a people through their force and
ideology. In Europe a considerable portion of the
populace is not as hardened against Communism as
we are. Therefore, in propaganda terms the Russians
could be more direct and forthright, and so they were.
The building was big, crass and vulgar, a semi-monu-
mental design of dimly seen classical origins. Inside
were the symbols of giantism. Everything that could
be was larger than life size, from the huge statue of
Lenin to a not-quite-life-size cutaway model of the
Tupolev transport, all of this dominated by models
of the first Sputnik. Their art exhibit was filled with
huge naturalistic illustrations of Soviet-type history.
The craftsmanship and design of most of the artifacts
shown were shoddy. But through it all one sensed a
serious and driving purpose. The symbols of their
rapid growth and power were carefully chosen, always
directed at the central ideas expressed by the concepts that Russia was big, it was powerful, it was
to be reckoned with. This was power politics through
symbolism. There was nothing to appeal to an esthete,
but to people looking for the symbols of the future
this was either a threat or a promise. Over all was the
impression that this was a nation vitally interested
in supremacy.

In comparison with the brash, vulgar, if forthright
Russian building the pavilion of the U.S.A. was a
negative statement made with elegant taste and esthetic discernment. It may have been an outright

mandarin choice, or perhaps the choice of symbols was motivated by the feeling that we were resented for our good fortune and power, and so the exhibit carefully avoided anything that would give offense to already quickened pride. But by so studiously avoiding anything that would give offense, we arrived at a pretty exhibit which hardly developed any of the manifest virtues of this country. It in some instances stressed isolated qualities, important only in association with our totality, but frivolous when alone.

Taken by themselves as designs and omitting any consideration as communication, the exhibit had some handsome things. The building was easily the most beautiful at the fair. Delicate, shimmering and graceful, it was a testament to our emerging delight with the mastery of structure. But the building, its purpose and use as a basis for communication were not integrated. The choice of the exhibit material seemed motivated toward attracting attention with little communication purpose in mind. One even wondered for whose attention the exhibit was directed—toward the already convinced, or perhaps for the applause of esthetic critics at home.

As a case in point, the main tent attraction was a fashion show. Beautiful girls periodically sauntered down to a platform in the middle of a pool located in the center of the building. The spectators stood around the edge of the pool and looked on. Since it is a proven fact that the world loves a pretty girl, from Rheingold drinkers to those who might be interested in a Chris-Craft, the spectacle was moderately well attended. But to what national purpose?

Around the exhibit were scattered a diverse array of isolated and rarefied objects, rarefied indeed when taken as symbol elements within the American society. One such that stays in my mind was a dummy mannequin dressed in a football player's uniform, lying prone in the manner of a dead crusader. The legend attached announced this as the uniform of a modern knight.

The official art chosen for display was almost entirely restricted to the then current school of action painters, representative perhaps as American painting to the selectors of the exhibit, but omitting other kinds of painting with appeals to a wider segment of society.

One exhibit which symbolized something directly related to the American spirit of technology and industry was a display of IBM computers and associated equipment. But by and large, with the exception of such isolated examples, the symbols chosen gave a negative impression of the U.S.A. Instead of the image of a vigorous leader of the free world, the impression was frivolous, almost effete.

It is not to be inferred from the examples chosen that an exhibit which chooses to use beauty or a light or ironic touch is necessarily a bad national propaganda platform. The problem lies rather in the choice of the symbol within the frame of reference. For symbols have associative impact differing with the experiences of those who see them. But the problem is even more deeply vested in the concept of the idea to be communicated, for it is the idea which controls the choice of one of the most powerful tools of communicating—the symbol.

Architectural form in building and exhibit has the power to embody the symbol to be communicated in its housing. This is true in the design of any building, for whatever purpose. It is as true for buildings which have a religious, institutional or corporate idea as it is in a fair. At a fair the purpose is more directly applied.

Part **5**

The Mandarins

The motivations for collecting probably are no different now from when the agents for Mellon, Morgan and Havemeyer ranged Europe and Asia ferreting out art masterpieces for their principals to acquire. The same personal drives exist, the same need to dress up the stage for a style of living with the appropriate props, the same desire to establish a posture and prestige through the ownership of tangible symbols of culture—a praiseworthy way of indulging an acquisitive hunger, plus the joys of the hunt, pursuit and discovery—in rarer instances, now as then, a desire to satisfy a craving for beauty, although it is difficult to identify much of the art collected today with beauty.

All of these motivations obviously have counterparts in both generations, but something new has been added. The older collectors were buying accredited, long-held masterpieces. The wealthy buyers had personal experts and advisors, like Berenson or Duveen, and followed an age-old tradition of collecting older art masterpieces, a tradition which had an unbroken continuity from Roman emperors through popes, Medicis, princelings, the barons of the *Almanach de Gotha* to the robber barons of their day. But in recent years the cream of the hunt has been to find unknowns, to be the first to buy them, to buy them cheaply, and then to bask in the refulgence of public acknowledgment of an act of discovery.

One would expect this kind of collecting to contain a sense of esthetic adventure which stands close to the borders of creativity. Is not the early recognition of an unestablished painter or sculptor an indication of sensitivity and perception second only to that of the artist himself? Unquestionably many present-day collectors possess such qualities, yet the business of contemporary art is so organized that these esthetic qualities really are not necessary.

For one thing, the values which make a contemporary collection noteworthy today are subjective and based on an entirely new set of standards. Second is the present state of the art market. Where before the collectors were making their choices from rarities which had an established order of desirability, rank and value, today the collector chooses from a scene crowded with many artists and works crying for attention. The collector operates within an enormous and continuing production. Before, there was a gauge of excellence between two works of the same period. Now the work is so defiantly original that the normal parameters of judgment disappear and one must rely on wholly subjective opinions.

The art which made up the body of earlier collections had time on its side. The opinions of centuries had been built by previous collectors. The bibliography was complete and extensive. The art had been hallowed by history. Now art tastes change rapidly. The *dernier cri* lasts a decade, more or less. Things move so rapidly that even the example of the impressionist collector is not good enough. While they are the incentive model for modern collectors, even in their case it took too long for the collections to reach public eminence. Things must move more rapidly now. We want action.

In order for a collection to become noteworthy in a compressed period of time, two things must happen. To start with last things first, the items in the collection, or companion pieces, must receive public acknowledgment from an authoritarian body, and in order to insure that the collection will contain works potentially worthy of such acknowledgment, it must be guided by a recognition of trends along correct channels.

Many instrumentalities exist in the art establishment today which insure such an outcome. On 53rd Street in New York City exists a Codex and Curia in a vatican called the Museum of Modern Art. Scattered through New York are the priests and acolytes who serve at its high altar, the art dealers, and located in major cities of the United States are the diocesan extensions of the Museum of Modern Art, independent museums in control, action and finance, but tied to the mother museum by esthetic cords.

The mandarin complex is composed of individuals and institutions. The operators of this group are reported in the press from time to time and form an illuminating account of the influences at work.

A story which appeared in *The New York Times* on July 2, 1963, concerned the auction of the collection belonging to Larry Aldrich, the New York dress manufacturer. His reported attitudes probably do not reflect those of many collectors who may not share Mr. Aldrich's sense of daring and adventure, but what he said does reflect the underlying motivation behind much of the collection and support of contemporary art.

The story relates that "the owner feels it [the collection] is not modern enough." Among the pieces being auctioned were an early Picasso which foretold the artist's cubist period; "The Washerwoman" by Gauguin; and one of Monet's beautiful water-lily pieces. Included as well were works by masters of the modern movement, paintings, sculptures, recognized as key stages in the development of important phases. To Mr. Aldrich these belong to an illustrious past. They have become the old masters of the modern movement, classics that offer no challenge in acquisition and no excitement in their pursuit. Mr.

Aldrich confessed that while he found the older works "pallid," making up his mind to sell them was a "soul-searching business."

Greater than his desire to continue in his possession of such an exemplary collection was his urgency to indulge his collector's instinct according to the new rules of the game. Collecting art fresh off the easel has become a "kind of a game." The manifest rewards lie in spotting new directions, pinpointing the best practitioners and acquiring their works at the right price. He said he had stopped "playing the game" with some artists because they had become successful and expensive; the game was spoiled. For some years he has provided $10,000 annually to the Museum of Modern Art for purchase of the works of artists not already in the museum's collection.

Contemporary art and the business of successful collecting has become so broadly publicized that books have been published advising the readership how to buy art wisely—from the point of view of investment rather than of beauty.[1] Homer Page of *The National Observer,* in discussing modern art and the average collector, stimulated his readers by telling of spectacular art value increases—a Jackson Pollock purchased in 1956 for $3,000 was now on sale for $100,000; a Paul Klee bought in 1939 for $165 was now valued at $16,000—and then dashed cold water on the kindled enthusiasm by warning that a John Singer Sargent water color purchased at $20,000 in the

[1]Richard V. Rush, *Art As An Investment* (Englewood Cliffs: Prentice-Hall, 1961).

1920s recently was sold for a mere $1,000.[2] Which are the John Sargents of tomorrow is a nagging question!

Such a broad-based interest in contemporary art is wonderful, even if the élite resent the intrusion of the great unwashed and some of the reasons for collecting lack the expected esthetic motivations. Newspaper periodicals and the fashion industry have all helped spread the new word about modern art, but the fountainhead, the source from which all blessings flow, is unquestionably the Museum of Modern Art in New York City, once called the fur-lined museum by Emily Genauer, the perceptive and independent art critic, after it had exhibited a pure surrealist sculpture composed of a fur-lined cup and saucer.

The Museum of Modern Art is an extraordinary, unique and paradoxical instrument for the propagation of culture, possessing the highest esthetic standards and power. It hurries into esthetic judgment because of its urgency to represent the new. It often bestows blessing and recognition on works or even on schools, without thought to their lasting value, as though it were a casual individual indulging his passing taste. It is a strange admixture of hallowed institution and fashion showcase. Its shows are presented with utmost seriousness surrounded by all the panoply of dramatic exhibit techniques and supporting publications, but its *vernissages* are like café society openings. The personalities and dress are reported on the fashion pages of the morning newspaper at the same time that the show is discussed in the art

[2]*The National Observer,* February 18, 1963.

column. The museum is intent on bringing contemporary art to the understanding of the public, but at times does it in terms that make understanding impossible. Amongst the treasures of absurd and pompous explanation which often accompany the exhibits is this gem contributed by the artist Ad Reinhardt himself, as quoted from *Time* magazine in a review headed "Ad Absurdum":

Among the new acquisitions currently on display at Manhattan's Museum of Modern Art is a large square canvas called "Abstract Painting" that seems at first glance to be entirely black. Closer inspection shows that it is subtly divided into seven lesser areas. In a helpful gallery note at one side, Abstractionist Ad Reinhardt explains his painting. It is: "A square (neutral, shapeless) canvas, five feet wide, five feet high, as high as a man, as wide as a man's outstretched arms (not large, not small, sizeless), trisected (no composition), one horizontal form negating one verticle form (formless, no top, no bottom, directionless), three (more or less) dark (lightless), noncontrasting, (colorless) colors, brushwork brushed out to remove brushwork, a mat, flat, freehand painted surface (glossless, textureless, nonlinear, no hard edge, no soft edge) which does not reflect its surroundings—a pure, abstract, nonobjective, timeless, spaceless, changeless, relationless, disinterested painting—an object that is self-conscious (no unconsciousness), ideal, transcendent, aware of nothing but art (absolutely no anti-art)."[3]

It is this kind of approach to its responsibilities, to the public and to art which at times seems to negate the value, extraordinary force and vision which the Museum of Modern Art has brought to its purposes. Opinions critical of the museum have begun to ap-

[3]*Time,* January 11, 1963.

pear with greater frequency. Most of them, while acknowledging the museum's general good judgment, take it to task in certain specific areas. The fault generally is found in the museum's predilection toward extremists. In the *Christian Science Monitor* review of "Americans 1963," Dorothy Adlow wrote:

The Museum of Modern Art presentations tend to be hospitable to the extremist. Thus, they provide us with an opportunity to follow in the wake of the frontiersmen; also to witness the swelling arrogance of some vanguardists, as well as the overextension of small ingenuities. What with the artist today snorting at tradition, rejecting amenities of technical accomplishment, adapting materials of shoddy or ephemeral character, pressing to exasperating extremes, it is a test and trial of critical balance to estimate the relative qualities of artistry among the trailblazers, to separate the sheep from the goats, to discriminate between the germane and the trivial.[4]

Mr. Stuart Preston in *The New York Times,* November 25, 1962, had previously voiced the same kind of sentiment anent the museum's practice of identifying experimental work with that which is most vital and to the point today, and concluded with, "One looks hard for paintings or sculpture that attests to delight in ordinary sensuous experience; in attempt to reconcile life and art instead of alienating one from the other."

In the same vein Emily Genauer in the *Herald Tribune,* May 1963, blamed the museum for its failure in earlier years to give a one-man exhibition to a sculptor like Rodin. She objected to the museum's

[4]Reprinted by permission from *The Christian Science Monitor* © 1963 The Christian Science Publishing Society. All rights reserved.

statement in the Rodin show announcement that during the '30s and '40s Rodin was ignored by artists and critics. If a powerful force for taste such as the museum itself can be preoccupied with transitory things and find time in its productive, influential 34-year history to choose rather to give one-man exhibitions to sculptors like Nadelman, Flannagan, Gonzalez, Gabo, Pevsner and others, but never one to Rodin, critics can hardly be held accountable for his present obscurity, was the burden of her charge.

Sounding a more acerbic note, John Canaday in his review on May 26 of the "Americans 1963" show, wrote:

On the whole, I do not think it is safe to take the museum's new show too seriously. For one thing, if you take it very seriously, you are bound to hold reservations concerning much of it, and that always hurts the museum's feelings and gets its staff involved in writing letters of explanation and defense that are too long to publish. We must remember that like the seed catalogues—this simile just won't down—the show is bright and promising and is planned like any other good promotional venture to get you pleasurably wrought up about the new items, which are always bigger and brighter than last year's, but does not guarantee that the current novelties will prove immune to the same nasty bugs that always get into the garden just when it looks most promising.[5]

The core of the reason for this growing volume of criticism is the fact that the museum is caught on the horns of a dilemma—a dilemma of purpose, the execution of that purpose and the role which is being forced upon the museum in this day and time, which it seemingly is unwilling to recognize. In his preface to the program of the tenth anniversary exhibit in 1939, the president, Mr. A. Conger Goodyear, re-affirmed the purposes of the museum. It was to be primarily an educational institution adhering to the policies of holding temporary exhibitions, illustrating the art of that day and its derivatives. This was a simple, straightforward explication of its purpose in the first ten years of its existence, valid and important for its time and place.

By the time of its fifteenth anniversary show in 1944, the museum had obviously become aware that its choice of contemporary art was beginning to arouse questions. It was growing in importance as an influence in art circles. In the foreword to the program which accompanied that anniversary show, it felt compelled to redefine its purposes:

No one connected with the Museum of Modern Art feels any prejudice or fanaticism for or against any branch or aspect of the progressive arts of our time. . . . [It] does not propose to be the final arbiter of the relative importance and accomplishment of the various schools of thought about art or of the different conceptions of modern beauty . . . neither is it a complacent repository of established values. It is rather a center of artistic life, to indicate the inspiration of the vigorous protagonists of the living arts and to clarify the beliefs and sensibilities which animate them.[6]

Today the museum, seemingly making itself oblivious to the enormous power it wields in the establishment of values and tastes, still adheres to a policy

[6]Fifteenth-Anniversary brochure of the Museum of Modern Art, New York, 1944.

which can no longer be operative at a time when the elementary educational tasks are completed and the art public needs another basis of exposition in order to arrive at a judgment. The essentially mandarin tastes of those who choose where and upon whom the museum will lay its hands indicate a careless, even naive, use of power. The fact that it is possible in a few short years to increase the sale value of a Jackson Pollock from $3,000 to $100,000 by sponsorship, and then inferentially have the power by equally impulsive neglect to deflate the value in a decade or two as was possible in the case of the John Singer Sargent, shows a lack of responsibility to its inherent powers.

Not that the museum can be accused of contriving to create the values from which the wheeler-dealers of the art world derive so much benefit. It is above such mercenary involvement, and yet the effects are precisely the same as though it were involved.

In its stated purpose of education the museum does not even begin to fill a role today. As an instance, how can anyone establish a basis for esthetic judgment between the values in the works of, say, Andrew Wyeth and Robert Rauschenberg? What aid or illumination does the museum furnish in helping a member of its audience to arrive at an informed opinion? There must be a way of accomplishing such ends without taking sides. These are not the sorts of questions that bother the museum; they only bother the art public. The museum is concerned with novelty, surprise and shock. It approaches the presentation of art as though it were a monthly magazine in search of a succession of big circulation builders. "Last month's edition is dead, what can we do now?" it seems to say.

In order to present the kind of work that interests its curators, it establishes an exotic basis of criteria for choosing art. Again, a quote from recent newspaper criticism is an indication of the belief that the museum authorities refuse to recognize a responsibility which they may disavow, but which nevertheless is being thrust upon them. Irving Sandler, in *The New York Post,* January 7, 1962, stated:

The Recent Acquisitions are dreary because the Modern did not choose them solely on the basis of quality. Other criteria entered: international coverage (half of the artists are American; the rest come from 25 countries); proportional representation of different styles (of the exhibits dating from 1957–1961, 26 are abstract; 16 are semi-abstract and 20 are clearly figurative); youth fetishism (one-quarter of the artists are under 35 years of age). Moreover, the museum was also concerned with predicting (or influencing) the course of contemporary art. Alfred H. Barr states that he is "not surprised that only three of the 23 artists under 35 . . . paint as abstract expressionists." Why "not surprised"? He is, after all, the director of the museum's collections, and largely responsible for the selections.[7]

Despite the growing impatience with its operations in mandarin tastemaking, the museum goes right ahead fulfilling its own manifest destiny. A final newspaper comment from John Gruen of the *Herald Tribune,* reviewing the pop art show:

[7]Reprinted by permission of *New York Post.* Copyright 1962, New York Post Corporation.

Every few years artists and galleries alike become ever so restless in the knowledge that the Museum of Modern Art is once again preparing for a big group exhibition. The questions begin to fly, "Who's going to be in it?"; "Who's going to be left out?"; "What faction will be favored?"; "Is pop art in?"; "Will they even touch abstract expressionism?"

The fever mounts as the museum official appointed to do the selecting quietly and noncommittally makes a tour of galleries, consults with dealers and makes his decisions. Pretty soon the word spreads. "Rosenquist is in, but not Lichtenstein!" "Marisol made it, and so did Bontecou!" "And Richard Lindner, why he's past 60!" and "Who the heck is Sally Hazelet Drummond?"

While in the last years the museum has flirted with neo-realist or pop art, it did not fully commit itself until now. Pop art runs rampant on the museum walls, shedding its "Walt Whitman-ia" all over the place. There's a room of Robert Indiana, a room of Claes Oldenberg, a room of James Rosenquist and one of Chryssa. In stating that the exhibit is not designed to illustrate a trend, Mrs. Miller seemed to imply that pop art has been around for eons, and its inclusion should come as no surprise to anyone. Surprising or not, the coveted stamp of approval has now been firmly placed on the "art of sat-on bananas" and its place in the art world is apparently established. . . . "Americans 1963," then, are the painters and sculptors that the Modern Museum feels strongly about. If their exposure will contribute to a richer, more absorbing art experience for the public, the museum will have done its duty. Our guess is that the show will confuse the public—leaving it torn between the instant accessibility of neo-realism—and the overly experimental plateaus reached by most of the other artists represented.[8]

Painting and sculpture have grown to be rarefied

[8]New York *Herald Tribune,* May 26, 1963.

experiences and it is the custom now to create an additional area of mystification by obscure interpretation and language. In an area that is more intimately related to real human experience and use the museum carries on the same, not-of-this-world attitude. This is seen in its exhibition of industrial design. For the main part, the choice of the decorative artifacts of living, the glassware, the silver, china, and the selection of the utilitarian goods with which our life is crowded follow the current avant-garde levels of taste. It cannot, however, in places resist imposing quixotic decisions of taste divorced from logic, the technical truths of a machine age, and the economic facts of life. In the selection of objects that are designed for use, it carries over the same mandarin approach that forms its taste in painting, sculpture and architecture.

At one time, the tastes of the selectors ran to the rigid geometric forms found in the then popular international style of architecture. When it came time to choose an electric toaster as an example of good design, they naturally chose one in which the form approximated their architectural ideal. It was a cube of shiny metal with the two normal slits which accommodate the bread slices in its top.

The electric bread toaster which was currently on sale in every store across the land was rejected as a bad design, since it was a curvilinear, soft shape. The curved shape of the skin happened to be the best engineering and production solution to the problem. It was a simple drawn shape, fitting over a base which contained the mechanism. It was easy to manufacture and therefore cheaper. In addition, it was easy to keep clean; the top, being curved, provided no resting place for the crumbs which inevitably result. It had no joints in which dirt and dust could gather and adhere.

The cube shape, on the other hand, was a far less logical manufacturing solution. In order to create a cube with sharp corners, the top was a crisply stamped shape which fitted over a drawn rectangular side wall. The top, being flat and level, was a gathering place for dust and crumbs. The manufacturing processes inevitably made it more expensive. There was not a whit's difference in the way it toasted the bread. However, the one the museum's curator chose did resemble the cube house so popular at the moment. It had been chosen because the selector had not been picking an object for utilitarian use which best met the problem. Instead of recognizing that the esthetic for such an object best grows from the facts of its use and manufacture, he was indulging his taste in sculpture and architecture-borrowed esthetics.

In a closed seminar at the museum on the occasion of another Design for Use show, a visiting professor-critic held the opinion that the museum was consistently a proponent of gee-whiz design. An example of such gee-whiz ardor was on exhibit in the room below. It was the removed back wiring panel of an IBM computer. It consisted of serried rows of brightly colored spaghetti tubing. Any act of creativity of design had been accomplished long before this panel was assembled. That act of technical magic had been performed by the engineer who laid out the wiring diagram; he did not choose the color; the colors were an accident of the logic of circuiting. The resulting assemblage, however, must have been reminiscent of string paintings, constructivist sculpture and the accidental textural delights which emerge when they are isolated from the main body or surface of which they are a part.

The next step in this sort of logic of selection of objects of good design for use will be to take micro-photographic enlargements of the surface of a brushed metal container and thereby show the magnificent order and logic of minute indentations possible in a well-ordered technical society—beauties which unfortunately are hidden from the human eye.

It probably is unfair to damn the museum for its refusal to recognize and use the power it has attained with more restraint and responsibility. Our culture and contemporary art would have been poorer if it never had done the magnificently vigorous job of education which it set out to do, and did in such a lively manner. The responsibility we expect from the museum now would make the job more difficult and certainly less fun than tripping happily along through the field of art's daisies. Yet, in a democratic society, we look for responsibility in all segments of our leadership group. With power, unfortunately, comes responsibility.

The power of the Museum of Modern Art as a taste-setter is felt throughout the country. Through many instrumentalities and communication devices, contemporary art has become ultra-fashionable. The fashion magazines use objects of art as backgrounds for their projection of coming fashion; if not the object itself, then some approximation of its esthetic, adapted to the purpose of selling dresses, coats and furs.

The shelter magazines are devoted to the propagation of the word about contemporary art and architecture. Even those which resist some of the more avant-garde aspects, as being entirely alienated from human needs, cannot avoid inclusion of many examples, else they would look old hat and fuddy-duddy. The shelter sections of the weekly news magazines, which have little use for the shelter idea other than as lively reportage, generally choose the most outrageous examples. These examples naturally have the greatest shock value and therefore are the most newsworthy. They broadcast the idea that these examples are wider-spread in acceptance than they really are. As a matter of fact, the more outrageous the example, the more likely it is to get space in the large national magazines. Clever tract developers, recognizing this phenomenon, take advantage in a manner that would have made P. T. Barnum envious. A housing developer in Florida got momentary national attention by building a house upside down, furnishing it and opening it to public view.

Another new entry as propagandist for the new esthetic, or rather a user of the communication mediums which are available when contemporary art is the subject, is certain large corporations which use art to establish an image of forward thinking, selfless philanthropy and involvement in the community good. These elements certainly are present and contain tax benefits as well. These corporations have put up monumental structures as their headquarters buildings. The cost of the structures often is two-to-three times that of a building which is erected as an ordinary real estate venture. These buildings would be an economic impossibility if expected to earn their keep in the rigors of a free enterprise economy. The differential is made up by using part of the public relations budget.

The City of New York has just had the indelicacy to suggest that since this is the case, the building should be appraised for tax purposes at its true value rather than at an arbitrarily arrived-at figure. It makes the burden that much more, but it has not seemed to affect the rate of building this kind of prestige structure, and it would be most unfortunate if it did. An increasing number of corporations have gone into the business of collecting art and putting the exhibits on display as a cultural extension of their regular public relations program. The collections, the art on display in their new building, are all used for guided tours through the headquarters buildings as well.

These all are useful and laudable activities. They have a praiseworthy cultural impact on the community. The only questionable element is the effect it has on art itself. Since newsworthiness is at such a high premium, excesses of originality are bound to be encouraged to the exclusion of other, perhaps more contemplative, searches.

Another recent entry in the lists of those who are building showcase architecture are certain universities.

They are not impelled by any mercenary reasons. This is being done for the greater glory of the university by identifying it with what is new and forward, that is, if that really should turn out to be the case.

Over the years there has been a great deal of critical dissatisfaction expressed with the functioning of existing university buildings. These either had been inspired by college buildings of older European universities, or built in the style current in the United States at the time of their planning. While in the first case the result gave a romantic impression of scholasticism, the kind of space derived from both was dark, inflexible and inadequate. Therefore, there is every functional reason for a change. In addition, every college building must have been of a new style at one time or another, including those at Oxford, so that it certainly is within the university tradition to support new styles of architecture.

What is disturbing is that the choices today are being made from the extremist, transitional wing of designers and not constrained to any one kind at that. Campuses become dotted with contemporary showcases of differing styles which, because of their design content, often offer functional problems of their own. Many of these buildings are handsome, some beautiful, some just exhibitionist, but beyond appearance there is little harmony between one new building and another, and certainly none with the older ones already in existence. In some instances, where the siting permits isolation, the buildings do not trouble the total complex. But most campuses unfortunately are full. We are presented with a disturbing break in the tone of architectural cohesiveness and of scholastic objectivity which one hopes to feel in the precincts of a university system.

This all may be thrust aside as a matter of taste. On the other hand, the idea of a university is that of a continuing center for learning. It can house diverse opinions and beliefs, although one expects that these will be presented with an objective point of view. It has a duty to explore new ideas. However, it seems a far reach when a university takes to the hustings as a proponent of transitional styles, especially while they are still in an unsettled transition. The trouble is that the exhibits are so permanent, and the ambiance of a campus is a precious ideal, not to be identified with a world's fair ground or a commercial center.

This architectural method of identification with the new is only an outward manifestation of a far more important conviction. It is in the teaching of architecture that the desire to be identified only with the *dernier cri* really has a far-reaching effect. In many universities it has become the thing to engage a practicing architect who is blessed with unilateral and didactic views. He rarely gets time from his practice and other external commitments to have much contact with the student body. In effect, he represents a point of view. The teaching is left to his assistants. The unhappy quality of this system is that the products of such an education become a conditioned group whose hands and hearts have been guided along narrow channels of architectural expression and thought, with a difficult adjustment to make when they go unprotected into the world outside.

It may seem unfair and unreasoning to hold up to criticism the actions of corporations, universities, institutions or individuals for their support of contemporary art. Certainly taking anyone to task for acts which are philanthropies and seem to be in the public interest would be unreasoning and thoughtless unless one were concerned that (a) a principal reason for doing so is its newsworthiness and that (b) this very newsworthiness is a destructive element for art.

Since a great deal of the newsworthiness comes from the striking originality of a given work, any self-questioning on the part of an artist is blunted. With this much assurance being piled upon him, any hesitation is eliminated. The artist has indicated from time to time that he is aware of the growing alienation between his art and man, but the nature of the support he receives for his adventures in cloud cuckoo land insulates him from criticism, and even more from the occasional restiveness he betrays when faced with the conglomerate effect of his own product.

We have seen an attitude toward the separation of man and art which came into being slightly more than a century ago gain in momentum. This attitude was first restricted to the artist. It gradually came to include the esthete and then an isolated part of a sophisticated public. It now has become widespread, so that any number can play. The attitude, joined with other social phenomena, is applying strong alienating pressures to society. When art becomes a clan symbol for an élite, the mandarins, its historic relationship to man is altered and its future purposes become less clear.

The Dilemma of Choice

Artists face in our time a crisis of choice far more acute than any they have ever known before. In the simplest possible terms, a practitioner in any of the arts today finds himself facing a choice between being an artist responsible only to his art, and being a man responsible to other men.

The need to make a choice, or a compromise of choice, has grown as his artistic attitude toward society has gone from a defiant nose-thumbing at a Philistine middle class in reaction to disillusionment, to a point where the complete separation between man and art is near at hand. The artist and his mandarin friends have turned art into a sacred icon, a thing apart, to be kept inviolate from the indecencies of living. It is worshipped by an over-ritualized cult where the dedication to the ritual idea has obscured the godhead. The worship of HOW has blotted out WHY and WHO.

Man the non-artist is left without any choice to make. He is outside. He looks at the frenzied action in art from a great distance. It is like a galactic explosion, rushing through a limitless void, possessed of enormous power and force, but alone in its dark orbit. It can be closely observed by those with lenses powerful enough to see it and who care enough to attempt an interpretation. If there is a purpose it is difficult to relate it to the world of men. The lack of purpose and relationship is outlined at the outset of Maritain's essays on the *Responsibility of the Artist*. He quotes André Gide as saying, "To be able to think freely, one must be certain that what one writes will be of no consequence."

To understand how this gifted artist, or any artist, can find it possible to free himself from any responsibility to, and relationship with, the living experience, we can compare his present role with that which was played by the artist in the past. Ortega y Gasset offered this comparison:

The artist has come from a position where he was involved with activities of enormous caliber. Art was expected to take on itself nothing less than the salvation of mankind. Art was important because it dealt with the profoundest problems of humanity and on account of its own significance as a human pursuit from which the species derived its justification and dignity, whereas a present-day artist would be thunderstruck if he were trusted with so enormous a mission. To his mind, the kingdom of art commences where the air feels lighter and things, free from formal fetters, begin to cut whimsical capers. . . . The symbol of art is seen again in the magic flute of the Great God Pan which makes the young goats frisk at the edge of the grove. . . . Other styles must be interpreted in connection with dramatic social or political movements or with profound religious and philosophical currents. . . . The new style only asks to be linked to the triumph of sports and games.[1]

The shift in the artist's position from involvement in large-caliber human activities to the whimsical triumph of sports and games has not been sudden, nor, for that matter, has the present position been reached entirely by lighthearted means. By and large the motivations have been attended by deep esthetic purposes. The trouble lies with these very esthetic purposes, for they do not seem to have much to do with man, and the attempt to serve both man and art is the heart of the dilemma for the artist.

The artist's dilemma is the subject of much discussion and thought. In a series of lectures[2] Jacques Maritain, the distinguished French Catholic, scholar, philosopher and humanist, developed the idea that the artist, a man, is confronted by two separate concepts— that of artistic value, which relates to his work, and that of moral values, which relate to his being a man. Maritain conceives these as two autonomous worlds,

[1]José Ortega y Gasset, *The Dehumanization of Art* (Princeton: Princeton University Press, 1948).

[2]Delivered at Princeton University. Published as *Responsibility of the Artist* (New York: Charles Scribner's Sons, 1960).

art and morality, each sovereign in its own sphere. The problem arises from the fact that these two worlds cannot ignore or disregard each other, for man belongs in these two worlds, both as an intellectual maker and a moral agent. His actions affect his own destiny. Therefore, since an artist is a man before being an artist, and is not an abstract impersonation of art come down from an Apollonian separate heaven, but is a man using art, the autonomous world of morality is superior to the autonomous world of art. "There is no law against the law on which the destiny of man depends."

The dilemma of the artist is one aspect of the larger dilemma which confronts the intellectual segment of the community of man. It pervades all areas of endeavor and is germane to most institutions and beliefs. C. P. Snow[3] has explored the widening gulf between the scientist and the humanist intellectual which has grown out of the dedication to the abstract ideal of science for science's sake. The most profound dilemma of all, man's continuing search for his identification with the concept of God, and the nonmystical, pragmatic, scientific rationale, has produced a new series of questions and ideas from Sören Kierkegaard's "either/or" to Martin Buber's "I, Thou and I." There is a continuing exploration into man's relationship to God and to men in the modern world. The less-trained and intellectually curious segments of society are no less aware of the ferment, but theirs is not so much

[3]C. P. Snow, *The Two Cultures and the Scientific Revolution* (New York: Cambridge University Press, 1959).

an intellectual awareness as it is intuitive and the fact
that they physically are affected by the loss of direction.

In pursuing the nature of the two autonomous
worlds, Maritain argues that the notion of an esthetic
or an artistic value has nothing to do with moral value.
"Art taken in itself tends to the good of the work,
while moral values relate to the good of man. A man
can be a great artist and be a bad man." For that matter, we do not care a hang that Gesualdo murdered
his wife, her suspected lover and the child which he
thought was not his. It now serves just as an exotic
footnote on the program when we listen to his music.
Or as Oscar Wilde, ever one for a startling epigram,
said, "The fact of a man being a prisoner is nothing
against his prose."

However, despite the fact that the good in art and
in morality are separate, the source for the action in
both lies in the exercise of the freedom of will and
choice made by a man who is an artist. As Maritain
puts it,

If human actions were mere events of nature resulting
from the interaction of the constellations of causes at work
in the world, there would be only the universe of nature—
there would be no ethical universe, no universe of morality.
But human actions are introduced into the world as the
result of a free determination, as something which depends on an initiative irreducible to the casual connections
at play in the whole world, and taken by another whole
which is myself, my own person, in such a way that I
am responsible for it. I myself am the author of my action,
be it good or bad.[4]

[4]Maritain, *loc. cit.*

Art has no being and therefore no intellect. It cannot be responsible. It is man, a particular man who thinks through his intellect in using art, who is morally responsible.

The melancholy irony is that in published statements[5] the artist is not unaware of this responsibility. He pays obeisance in passing to the unhappy fact that he, the artist, operates within an increasingly alienated society and claims for himself the role of one of the last defenders of the realm of the human spirit. He bemoans the lack of social goals and the sense of loss of historic participation. Having given voice to this melancholy recognition, he turns his back squarely upon these problems and devotes his energies toward asserting his need and right to develop his own private vision; a right which nobody seems any longer to contest or deny him. The private vision the artists seek now is a kaleidoscope of novel techniques and the envy of and desire to share the abstract, unassailable truths of science.

In Hermann Hesse's Nobel Prize novel, *Magister Ludi,* he writes of a community of an intellectual élite. They have perfected a mystical symbol language called the Bead Game, which has reduced all knowledge to a sort of unified field theory. The world outside the community rages with trouble, but the players of the Bead Game have lost all contact with common man. They are engaged in exchanging their esoterica with one another in the game. There is certainly a disquieting parallel when one reads of the goals and problems

[5]*Dædalus, Journal of the American Academy of Arts and Sciences* (Winter 1960).

uppermost in the artist's mind when he speaks of his goals in the exercise of his private visions. He speaks of space, the transcendence of space, the multiplication of space, the division and negation of space. It is a space devoid of men, as though they did not exist. It is, in fact, a version of the Bead Game.

If the artist recognizes the fact of an alienated society, there seems to be little sympathy for the fact that it is man who is estranged, not just an abstract deterministic system. When the energies and dreams of the artist are concentrated upon service to an abstract ideal which increases the force of alienation, then he is failing in his moral responsibility to man. When the elements of estrangement become strong enough to be a divisive force between man and art, then the artist who furthers this is failing in his responsibility to art.

There were much easier choices to make when Goethe expressed his concept of creative, experiential unity: "Religion, art and science satisy man's threefold needs for creation and for vision; all of these are one in the beginning and in the end, although distinct at the center." But since that serene statement the world has been busy tearing everything apart with very little time expended in rebuilding. All beliefs, social, religious, sexual or political, have been disjointed. The world is torn, negative, restless and revolutionary. We pick at the scabs of old wounds. There may have been more implied than said when Apollinaire remarked, "The artist of our time treats his object as a surgeon dissects a corpse."

The source for the dilemma of choice lies in the

continuing allegiance to the dogma "art for art's sake" In all probability, the artist's inner attitude toward art for art's sake has undergone some change. In a half-century that has felt the impact of technology, Marx, Freud and two devastating wars, it is now perhaps more a refuge and retreat than a flaming cause. None the less, it still is an operative attitude, whatever the artist's inner relationship may be. It is in this attitude that the heart of the conflict between the good of the work and the good of man lies. Maritain in his essays quotes from Yeats to make such a point:

The intellect of man is forced to choose
Perfection of the life, or of the work,
And if it take the second must refuse
A heavenly mansion, raging in the dark
When all that story's finished, what's the news?
In luck or out the toil has left its mark:
That old perplexity, an empty purse,
Or the day's vanity, the night's remorse.[6]

In further discussion of the point, he amplifies: "The motto 'art for art's sake' simply disregards the world of morality and the values and rights of human life. 'Art for art's sake' does not mean art for the work which is the right formula. It means an absurdity, that is, a supposed necessity for the artist to be only an artist, not a man, and for art to cut itself off from its own supplies and from all food, fuel and energy it receives from human life."[7]

Art has the power to move man. It reaches him through his intuition, his recognition and response to beauty, and through all of his senses and abilities. It

[6]From "The Choice" by W. B. Yeats.   [7]Maritain, *loc. cit.*

reaches him through his intellect, his imagination, passion and sensuous delight. Art alone is powerless; art through man has the power to move the community. Anything which can move man and the community to that degree has a responsibility to both.

In the awareness of that responsibility, can the community insist that the artist work for the good of the community? Should the needs of the community establish the rule for creativity and become, as Maritain poses, an art for *people's* sake? The answer must be no. For just as art for art's sake disregards the good of man, so an art for people's sake implies a disregard for the good of art. The fact remains that an artist is an artist. If he took for his rule the good of the community without regard to his duty to art he would become a propagandist and subject to the whim of the community rather than to the dedication to the values of the creative intellect. It would be an act of irresponsibility on the part of the community to dictate to the artist as well. It loses its dignity and sense of values when it exercises its power to dictate as in the act of banning *Ulysses* or *Lady Chatterley's Lover.*

The relationship of responsibility and morality in the arts is not just a contemporary concern. The question recurs from time to time but there is generally some element which makes the answers inapplicable as a working rule. The weakness in Tolstoy's definition of art as the communication of emotion lies in the gradation of excellence he imposed, for to him the higher the level of social morality the greater the work of art. Tolstoy makes the error of assuming that a social or moral value is the supreme standard of art.

It is only when a moral value is fully integrated with the artist's creative intellect that this is possible. It is so in Picasso's social reaction to Guernica. It is not so in a state-dictated art such as the Russian intentional glorification of Lenin and Stalin. The autonomous worlds of art and morality cannot disregard each other, and yet they must remain autonomous. This autonomy cannot be maintained when the ideals of truth and integrity are respected only in pursuit of esthetic goals; certainly not when these ideals are given facile lip service in support of an esthetic posture. The autonomy of art and morality can be based only in the artist's complete honesty to himself, to his art and to his being a man and therefore part of mankind.

There is little room for a Solomon's choice in a dichotomous allegiance to art and morality. There is a need for balance, but it cannot be imposed. There certainly is no easy solution at hand. Maritain discusses François Mauriac's ideas, which, while offering no complete solution, come close to a beginning when he calls for a "purification of the source." Such an act of purification calls for a rededication to human ideals as well as esthetic ideals. Mauriac recognizes his own difficulty in arriving at a creative choice in the present dilemma. "One would have to be a saint, but then one would not write novels," says he. Or, for that matter, be a poet, architect, painter or musician.

And finally, the artist has one ultimate responsibility to his art: it is to see that it survives. If we are to take seriously any of the lessons learned from history, then we must recognize that an art has the best chance of survival if it is a vital part of man's organic and esthetic experience. When art is used as an instrument to bludgeon man into a position of inferiority, used to set him apart and make him feel denied the sacrament of beauty, man may turn his back on the art we know. As Maritain says,

People cannot indefinitely bear to have their basic standards or beliefs mocked or undermined, their moral heritage threatened, their own minds confused or their imagination poisoned for the sake of the artist's irresponsibility. These reactions can be dull and queer, Philistine, misguided or simply coarse. They are a phenomenon of natural, so to speak, biological defense.[8]

Man is tenacious. In the long battle for survival it is he who has remained. In the process he has defeated enemies, discarded institutions, instinctively sought for and developed elements and factors within his society which have supported and enriched him, as part of his natural, intuitive defenses. His decisions are not made with lightning-stroke suddenness. There is rarely a sudden disappearance of the things that plague him, only a wasting atrophy. Art faces such atrophy, especially the art of the easel painter. The painter has been in flight from technological displacement for almost a half-century. The frightening power of photography as an instrument to record and to create out of reality cannot easily be overcome. The painter, in his flight from photography, sought ground on which photography could not immediately operate, but the gap is closing. In his flight to higher ground, isolation, mystery and obscurity became camp followers of the painter. It is difficult for a medium as ephemeral and

[8]*Op. cit.*

as obscure as present-day painting to maintain its conscious importance in the minds and hearts of men.

A great part of the respect and adulation given to art is due to art's heritage from the past. We treat with kindness and understanding a wayward son of a great man, partially closing our eyes to his attitudes or behavior. Like the wayward son of a past giant, painting is living off the capital of love created by its illustrious forebear. As a profession, it still is identified with the glories of the past. Man has a conditioned reflex to art. He feels he must respect it despite the fact that it is difficult for him to believe his own eyes. Some day he suddenly may become convinced that this emperor, too, has no clothes.

Painting faces a difficult future, especially with its current trends, because it is increasingly a private art. A painting of a religious experience which once created wide enthusiasm and interest today faces a medium in which more than one hundred million people simultaneously can see the coronation of a pope. The spectacle can further be recorded to be seen again and again. Malraux's concept of the museum without walls is expanding. It has enormous potential in making the art of the past a vital present. At hand are techniques for mechanically viewing and recording the masterpieces of the past from vantage points never before seen. On the verge of development are methods to project these dimensionally and in color. These projections will become a part of the intimate experience of men in their homes. These methods have inherently an enormous power to communicate beauty and mystery. The recording and broadcasting of music already is at the early stages of such a revolutionary development. A vast audience for art is being built by mechanical means.

Millions more will see and remember a book made into a movie than those who will ever read it. While at present these powerful mediums are overpopularized and their product unfortunately verges upon and sometimes achieves total vulgarity, the vulgarians are men, and men are subject to change. At the moment they seem to be pandering largely to the lowest tastes and desires of the public. The medium has no will of its own. It can change. England has her third program. We can have a seventh or a ninth.

In recognition of this ultimate responsibility to art, its survival, the artist cannot avoid making a choice out of the options which he is offered. The choice comes down to a viable direction for his future in art. We are on the threshold of even more revolutionary changes in our social and technical lives. These changes will emphasize a single aspect of the dilemma of choice, one that essentially centers on man. Shorn of all of the obvious shades of difference inherent in the potential, it comes down to this. In the face of an increasingly complex and alienated world, will the artist choose to retreat into an even more esoteric obscurity, happy in the commendation of a rarefied sect, or will he try to re-enter the mainstream of living?

There is no suggestion that choices will be offered in such clearly visible, black-and-white terms. For that matter, neither is the promise of cheap victories to be gained by crowd pleasing, commensurate with the highest ideals of honesty and integrity. And yet, in the truest term of these ideals, the artist will have to make some such choice.

It will not be easy to reverse the trend when we consider that in the background of that choosing is the century and a half of suspicion of public taste which has dominated the creative artist. It is open to question whether such a complete rejection is justifiable today when the public has indicated a willingness to be led, to be taught. To maintain an unbending and habitual attitude has more to do with the continuance of a caste system than with the uninhibited search for expression. There is no reason why the search cannot be conducted within the framework of public understanding as well as outside it. Also, there is no implication that the artist must pander.

It has been argued that the health and vitality of art are endangered by too much public understanding. The painter Gottlieb was most forthright in this opinion. Yet, in the long line of experience, and despite temporary shifts in taste and fashion, the innermost longings of men have been constant. In the responses to these urges can be found the roots and sources for much of the mythology, legend, music and poetry which are men's heritage of beauty. The first fulfillment of these human wants may appear in the form of a popular art or, to call it by a less elevated name, "popular entertainment." When such an art comes into being, it matters not what attitude the intellectual community has toward the art; its power and penetration are undeniable. Such popular arts have extraordinary ability to reach masses of men. Despite the fact that these arts may be greeted by indifference or scorn by the intellectual community, they often find their way into the cultural life of succeeding generations.

Consider two popular forms of entertainment which have had their origins in this country and in an astonishingly short space of years have penetrated to the far corners of the earth. The extraordinary pair I have in mind are jazz and motion pictures. Taken at their esthetic face value, one properly may wonder why these two popular arts should be considered alongside the arts which we consistently spell with a capital *A*. And yet, their power to communicate, penetrate and emotionally move large numbers of people cannot be readily shunted aside.

Both of these popular arts have come to international acceptance and are undergoing the formative stages of adaption to separated national coloration. What makes them worthy of consideration is not the potential they offer as inspiration to, or in combination with, other arts—a virtue which probably is nil; rather, what makes them engrossing is that in spite of all the early scorn heaped upon them as popular art, they have prospered and both are beginning to emerge as serious art forms, and as art forms they are providing a vehicle for many diverse artists to find their own individual kinds of expression.

Jazz has come an incredible distance in a half-century. It now is heard in the Concertgebouw Orkest of Amsterdam and in the concert halls of Moscow, Helsinki, Cairo, Bangkok and Tokyo. Despite the raging discussion of Jim Crow and Crow Jim now in progress between some white and colored jazz musi-

cians as to the relative merits in each kind of performance, it is interesting to note that while the music unquestionably had its origins with the Southern Negro,
its sources were not African music, but rather, European, in scale, harmony and instrumentation. Only the
rhythm is new, and while it has no visible antecedents
in Europe, neither can it be traced to Africa.

One of the qualities which gives present jazz so
much freshness is the spontaneity which comes through
individual and group improvisation. Curiously, this
spontaneity has been sought by the action painters
without commensurate success. In their case the improvisation takes place at the moment of the action,
but the result stares back, stolidly, unmoving and
repetitious. In jazz, it is a passing through, alive with
the spontaneity of constant change and movement.
Further, because of the changing base of melody and
rhythm, the endless repetitions are avoided.

Jazz is winning adherents, few of whom share the
ethnic problems or social history of its progenitors.
Having started in a most commonplace manner, jazz
slowly and impressively is gaining intellectual stature
and consideration as a serious art form. It is doing this
despite the seeming burden of popular support and
understanding.

Movies are advancing rapidly to the status of an
art while they still continue to penetrate every part of
the world as an escapist entertainment. The power of
this medium as a form of communication is so extraordinary that it is unavoidable that artists the world
over are moved to use it. Men with diverse national
backgrounds such as Akira Kurosawa from Japan,

Alain Resnais of France, Ingmar Bergman from Sweden, Andrzej Wajda of Poland, Leopoldo Torre Nilsson of Argentina and India's Satyajit Ray all have created works in which a universal concept or problem is embodied in a national point of view or vehicle. These productions are exchanged and shown all over the world. The "new wave" is coming to have a precise meaning in this country and the names of Fellini and Ingmar Bergman are almost common currency. Academies and festivals have arisen with the purpose of recognizing and rewarding artistic contributions.

The range of the medium is wide, so that it can contain introspective comments like Fellini's *8½*, Bergman's *The Silence*, spectacles like *Cleopatra* and *Becket* and a joyous romp like *Tom Jones*. Because, for the moment at least, the technique has been mainly to photograph elements of reality in whatever natural or surreal relationship, the impact is immediate and unavoidable, however obscure the comment. It promises an even greater future when the motion picture art finally is realized.

Man has surrounded his life with the telling of old legends and the invention of new ones. He relishes musical and dance creations through which he can give vent to his emotions. He adorns himself and his surroundings with color and decoration to enrich his environment. He stands in awe and fear at concepts of his origin and final disposition. In all things he responds to inner urges. However primitively they start, his desires for magic, beauty and poetry have converted phenomena of expression into art of one kind or another. If man is denied an art vitally identified with himself from one source, he will find it in another. The Bead Players who make themselves unconscious of the innate longings of men will be passed by and left to their game. They will join other fossil practitioners of a past art like armorers, fletchers, clipper shipwrights and Dada painters.

Whether the artist is an honest son of his time, capable of a lasting contribution, depends not so much on the imitation or rejection of the technological phenomenon, not on the applause of a mandarin coterie, but upon the fact that he has a responsibility not only to his art but to the men who live in his time as well. His time is complex and the task of interpreting it with clarity is difficult, yet the artist still can find direction in the aims set down by Joseph Conrad in the magnificent preface to *The Nigger of the Narcissus*. It is a statement that all artists can interpret for their own needs:

He [the artist] speaks to our capacity for delight and wonder, to the sense of mystery surrounding our lives; to our sense of pity, and beauty, and pain; to the latent feeling of fellowship with all creation—and to the subtle but invincible conviction of solidarity that knits together the loneliness of innumerable hearts, to the solidarity in dreams, in joy, in sorrow, in aspirations, in illusions, in hope, in fear, which binds men to each other, which binds together all humanity—the dead to the living and the living to the unborn.

The level of sophistication of art, added to the complexity of a contemporary message, considered against the face of the looming challenge of past art, undoubtedly calls for new ways by which the artist will reach men. He can insist that men follow where he leads, but only if he has any real desire that they follow. If at present he does not feel up to the task of leading them, he should at least desist in his mad efforts to escape from contact with them. The door marked SECRET KNOWLEDGE—DO NOT ENTER should be cracked open.

Such a beginning would go a long way toward the "purification of the source." The artist can help find a way out of the morass of doubt and self-hatred which besets our time. And perhaps he again will speak of beauty and love instead of being the constant mirror of despair. The artist has extraordinary powers with which to reach men, for he has equipped himself with a remarkable range of techniques and tools, although he has been using them carelessly. He has rid himself of many restraints and inhibitions. He must rid himself of the final inhibition, his distrust of man.

Bibliography

Auerbach, Erich, *Mimesis*. Princeton, N.J.: Princeton University Press, 1953; paperback reprint, Garden City, N.Y.: Doubleday & Company (Anchor), 1957.

Barrett, William, *Irrational Man*. Garden City, N.Y.: Doubleday & Company (Anchor), 1958.

Baudelaire, Charles, *The Mirror of Art*. Garden City, N.Y.: Doubleday & Company (Anchor), 1956.

Berenson, Bernard, *Aesthetics and History*. New York: Pantheon Books, 1948; paperback reprint, Garden City, N.Y.: Doubleday & Company (Anchor), 1954.

Blackham, H. I., *Six Existentialist Thinkers*. New York: The Macmillan Company, 1952; paperback reprint, New York: Harper & Row (Torchbooks), 1959.

Buber, Martin, *I and Thou* (second edition). New York: Charles Scribner's Sons, 1958.

Chase, Stuart, *The Tyranny of Words*. New York: Harper & Row, 1938.

Connolly, Cyril, *The Condemned Playground*. New York: The Macmillan Company, 1946.

———, *Enemies of Promise*. New York: The Macmillan Company, 1938; paperback reprint, Garden City, N.Y.: Doubleday & Company (Anchor), 1960.

G. G. Coulton, *Art and Reformation*. New York: Cambridge

University Press, 1953; paperback reprint (two volumes, *Medieval Faith and Symbolism* and *The Fate of Medieval Art*), New York: Harper & Row (Torchbooks), 1958.

Daedalus, Journal of the American Academy of Arts and Sciences. Winter, 1960, issue, "The Visual Arts Today."

Elsen, Albert E., *Rodin.* New York: Museum of Modern Art, 1963.

Feibleman, James K., *Aesthetics.* New York: Duell, Sloan and Pearce, 1949.

Fry, Roger, *Transformations.* Garden City, N.Y.: Doubleday & Company (Anchor), 1956.

————, *Vision and Design.* New York: Meridian Books, 1956.

Gaunt, William, *The Aesthetic Adventure.* New York: Harcourt, Brace & World, 1945.

Gilson, Etienne, *Painting and Reality.* New York: Bollingen Foundation, 1957; paperback reprint, New York: Meridian Books, 1959.

Gombrich, E. H., *Art and Illusion* (second edition). New York: Bollingen Foundation, 1961.

Gropius, Walter, *The Scope of Total Architecture.* New York: Harper & Row, 1955.

Hartog, Howard, *European Music in the Twentieth Century.* London: Penguin Books, 1961.

Heinemann, F. H. *Existentialism and the Modern Predicament.* London: A. & C. Black, 1953; paperback reprint, New York: Harper & Row (Torchbooks), 1958.

Hesse, Hermann, *Magister Ludi.* New York: Holt, Rinehart & Winston, 1949; paperback reprint, New York: Frederick Ungar Publishing Co.

Hodeir, André, *Jazz.* New York: Grove Press, 1956.

Huxley, Aldous, *On Art and Artists.* New York: Meridian Books, 1960.

Jarry, Alfred, *Ubu Roi.* New York: New Directions, 1961.

Juvenal, *Satires,* translated by Rolfe Humphries. Bloomington, Ind.: Indiana University Press, 1958.

Langer, Susanne K., *Problems of Art.* New York: Charles Scribner's Sons, 1957.

Maritain, Jacques, *The Responsibility of the Artist.* New York: Charles Scribner's Sons, 1960.

Michener, James A., *The Floating World.* New York: Random House, 1954.

Mumford, Lewis, *Art and Technics*. New York: Columbia University Press, 1952.

———, *From the Ground Up*. New York: Harcourt, Brace & World, 1957.

Mumford, Lewis, *The Transformations of Man*. New York: Harper & Row, 1956.

Ogden, C. K., and Richards, I. A., *The Meaning of Meaning*. New York: Harcourt, Brace & World, 1923.

Ortega y Gasset, José, *The Dehumanization of Art*. Princeton, N.J.: Princeton University Press, 1948; paperback reprint, Garden City, N.Y.: Doubleday & Company (Anchor), 1956.

Ozenfant, Amédée, and Jeanneret, C. E. (Le Corbusier), *La Peinture Moderne*. Paris: Les Editions G. Grès, 1924.

Panofsky, Erwin, *Meaning in the Visual Arts*. Garden City, N.Y.: Doubleday & Company (Anchor), 1955.

———, *Studies in Iconology*. London and New York: Oxford University Press, 1939; paperback reprint, New York: Harper & Row (Torchbooks), 1962.

Pearson, Hesketh, *The Man Whistler*. New York: Harper & Row, 1952.

———, *Oscar Wilde*. New York: Harper & Row, 1946.

Pennell, E. R. and J., *The Life of James McNeill Whistler*. London: William Heineman, 1909.

Praz, Mario, *The Romantic Agony*. New York: Oxford University Press, 1933; paperback reprint, New York: Meridian Books, 1956.

Raynal, Maurice, *Modern French Painters*. New York: Brentano's, 1928.

——— et al., *History of Modern Painting*. New York: Skira International Books, 1950.

Read, Herbert, *The Philosophy of Modern Art*. New York: Horizon Press, 1953; paperback reprint, Grove Press, 1955.

———, *The Tenth Muse*. New York: Horizon Press, 1958; paperback reprint, New York: Grove Press, 1958.

Rewald, John, *The History of Impressionism*. New York: Museum of Modern Art, 1961.

Rodman, Selden, *Conversations with Artists*. New York: The Devin-Adair Co., 1957.

Rosenberg, Harold, *The Tradition of the New*. New York: Horizon Press, 1959; paperback reprint, New York: Grove Press, 1961.

Seidenberg, Roderick, *Post Historic Man*. Boston: Beacon Press, 1957.

Selz, Peter, *The Work of Jean Dubuffet*. New York: Museum of Modern Art, 1962.

Shattuck, Roger, *The Banquet Years*. New York: Harcourt, Brace & World, 1955; paperback reprint, Garden City, N.Y.: Doubleday & Company (Anchor), 1961.

Snow, C. P., *The Two Cultures and the Scientific Revolution*. New York: Cambridge University Press, 1959; paperback reprint, expanded edition, New York: New American Library (Signet), 1964.

Sullivan, Louis H., *Kindergarten Chats*. New York: George Wittenborn, 1947.

Wilenski, R. H., *Modern French Painters*. New York: Harcourt, Brace & World, 1940; paperback reprint, New York: Random House (Vintage), 1960.

Whitehead, Alfred North, *Adventures of Ideas*. New York: The Macmillan Company, 1933; paperback reprint, New York: New American Library (Mentor), 1955.

Wright, Frank Lloyd, *The Future of Architecture*. New York: Horizon Press, 1953; paperback reprint, New York: New American Library (Mentor), 1963.

Index

William Snaith

Born in New York City in 1908, William Snaith studied architecture and painting at New York University, the École des Beaux Arts in Paris, and the Fountainebleau Academy of Fine Arts. He is now President of Raymond Loewy/William Snaith, Inc., design, research and planning organization, beginning his career in design in 1936 with Loewy. Mr. Snaith is well known on sports pages and in yachting journals, not only as a writer but as the owner and skipper of winning sail boats, each named "Figaro." In 1963 he won the King of Sweden Cup in the trans-Atlantic race to Sweden. A prolific painter, Mr. Snaith has had four New York exhibitions and has shown several times in the Whitney Museum Annual collection of American paintings, at Pennsylvania Academy and other museums, and is represented in many private collections here and abroad.

A third aspect of his life is civic and political. He has been Vice Chairman of the Board of Education and a member of the Board of Finance of Weston and was Chairman of the Democratic Town Committee. He lives in Weston, Connecticut with his wife and three sons.